# VISNOSTICS™

## Special Edition for Auto Sales

The Power of
VISualization DiagNOSTIC Statements™
A Neuroscientific Approach to
Communicating, Training, Selling, Marketing, and
Leading.

## Kimberlee Slavik

Illustrated by David A. Wiener
Foreword by Joseph Ingram, The Sales Genius

# DEDICATION

I dedicate all of my books to my wonderful clients for helping me understand how to make sales an honorable, respected, strategic, intelligent, and rewarding process.

# SPECIAL THANKS

Thank you to the readers of *Visnostic Selling* AND *Visnostics Special Edition for Real Estate* for helping them BOTH earn Amazon's "Hot New Release in Global Marketing!"

For all of the innovators and early adopters who had the insight to understand the power of Visnostics, who bravely championed Visnostic Workshops, and who radically changed their company's messaging because of it – THANK YOU & CONGRATULATIONS!

David Wiener, I hope these best-selling books finally puts you on the map as a famous artist! You have been a wonderful mentor and my treasured friend for over a decade now! Who would have thought that we would have this incredible partnership that day you became my new Sales Vice President?!

And to my husband – Thanks for not thinking I'm crazy for taking time off to write these books! I love you!

And finally, thank you to my son, Zachary Steele Slavik, for designing a SECOND book cover for me! You are my sunshine no matter how old you get!

# VISNOSTICS™ Special Edition for Auto Sales

*The Power of*
*VISualization DiagNOSTIC Statements*
*A Neuroscientific Approach to*
*Communicating, Training, Selling, Marketing, and Leading.*

Copyright © 2019 by Kimberlee Slavik
www.dynaexec.com
Illustrations by David A. Wiener
Foreword by Joseph Ingram

ISBN: 978-1-7331946-4-8
Library of Congress Cataloging-in-Publication is available.
Design & Layout by DynaExec
Published by DynaExec
Cover by Zachary Steele Slavik, CEO of Steele Cross Productions

Printed in the United States of America

# VISualization DiagNOSTIC Statements™ Defined

## *Visualization*
verb (used without object)
to recall or form mental images or pictures.

## *Diagnostic*
adjective
of, relating to, or used in diagnosis.
serving to identify or characterize; being a precise indication.

## *Statement*
noun
something stated.
a communication or declaration in speech or writing, setting
forth facts, particulars, etc.

Please note that this is a
Special Edition for Auto Sales.
This is an excerpt from *Visnostic Sales and
Marketing* which replaces *Visnostic Selling*.

# Table of Contents

# FOREWORD
## By Joseph Ingram, The Sales Genius

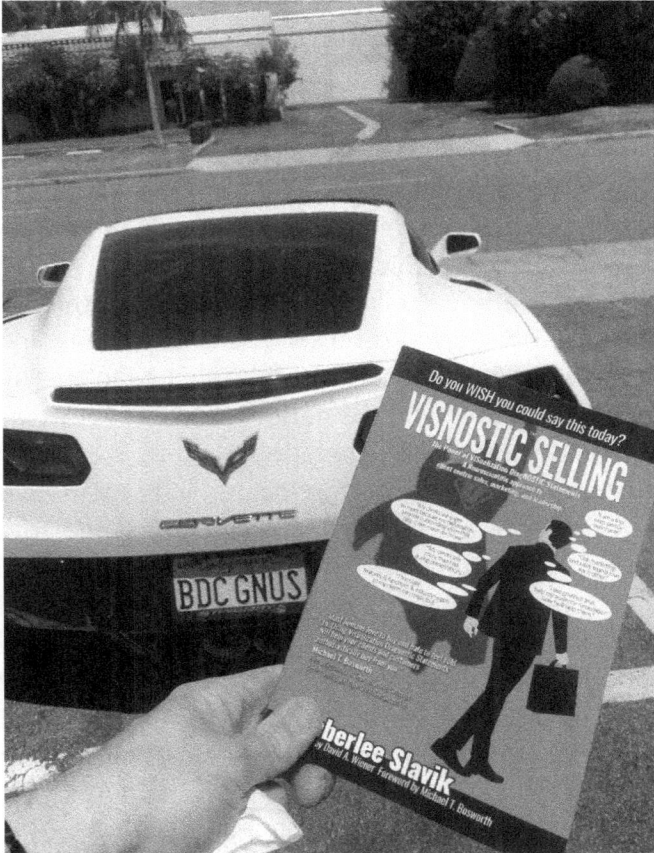

*"I am phenomenal at selling prospects a new or used vehicle."* If you WISH you could say this with 100% certainty, then this book is for you. You will increase your sales immediately by adopting and implementing the Visnostic selling system.

The automotive business has been my life and livelihood for the past 20+ years. Prior to officially joining a retail dealership I bought, repaired and sold vehicles for side cash. To say I love

1

cars is an understatement. When my parents gave me my first vehicle at the age of 16 years old, I started the get, fix and flip process. When I turned 17 years old I was on the 12th vehicle, yes I went through a car a month until I ended up with the car I wanted, a Chevy IROC Camaro.

**Auto enthusiast/ Car guy – CHECK!**

To say that I love the sales game is an understatement, and as most sales professionals I felt that I knew it all. I think when we get to the 3rd or 4th vehicle sold in a month we decided internally that we have this game mastered. Nothing can be farther from the truth. After 3 years of getting into the dealership world I was the General Sales Manager for the number 3 Toyota store in the nation. I took over at the 600 units per month mark, and throttled it up to 1,000 units per month. This was a single rooftop located in the worlds largest auto center, and we had tons of traffic and over 70 salespeople. At a time when the national average for a franchise store was 75 units per month, this was a feather in the cap moment. I later went on to become a GM of an independent used car lot by year 5 of my career. It was a brand new point, and it took us 90 days to hit 100 units sold per month. I then ventured into the sales training arena and worked with the greats, Joe, Grant, and Paul all of which were huge names in the automotive training space (and still are at the time of this writing), the only difference is I don't work for them anymore, I am their competition. I train many of the number one dealerships in the world on how to convert the virtual prospect into a sold vehicle. Utilizing my years of experience and gained knowledge on human psychology and buying triggers I have taken several dealerships to the 1,000 units a month as an employee or consultant.

**Sales Authority/Car guy – CHECK!**

Everything was going just fine when I happened to listen to a podcast with a lady named Kimberlee Slavik on it.

I was immediately taken back by her approach, and as you will find as you read this book, it's revolutionary, and pushes your mind to the limits of its preconceived ideas. I completed every exercise in the book, sent her my results, and engaged with her to expand my knowledge. I then began asking her guidance for Visnostic statement advice. I used her tutoring to land myself a $120k account n the automotive world. I sat in front of the CEO at the stretched out 18 person conference table in the corporate office in Chatsworth, CA. The first slide I put up was a Visnostic statement. The CEO read it, and yelled out "I WISH". I then clicked the next slide that offered everyone the choices 1. This is our current situation 2. I wish this was our situation and 3. This doesn't apply. The room erupted in laughter and the CEO turned to me and said – " if that was our current situation do you think we have you in here?" I never showed the slide with my accolades and talents or accomplishments. I got that account despite the other 4 companies that presented after me. The CEO told me after he signed my agreement that everyone else got up there and told us how great they were. *"You showed us we needed the help we knew we needed."*

That my friends is why you need to read this book multiple times. The car business is falling behind the times in its resistance to go digital and incorporate technology. Visnostic Selling is the best innovation in the automotive sales game in the last 100 years (I am only 52 years old, so the other 48 years was the result of a google search).

**Visnostic Selling Professional/Car guy – CHECK!**

Feel free to contact me directly if you have any questions joe@ingraminteractive.com

# REVIEWS*

## Of

## Kimberlee Slavik's Best Selling First Book,

## *VISNOSTIC SELLING*

## and

## TRANSLATION WORKSHOPS

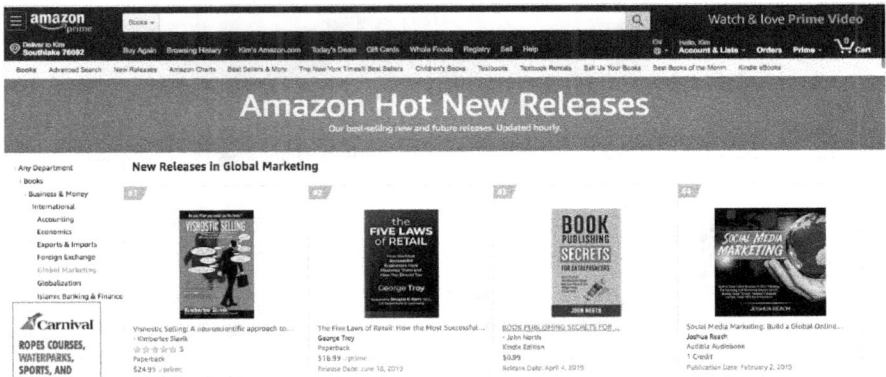

*\*Comments are from a diverse group of talent and experience including a Teacher, Politician, Visualization Expert, Direct Sales, Solution Architect, Channel Sales, Marketing, Ad Agency, Authors and Buyers. This book is written for everybody.*

Investing time to read this section of the book will help open your mind to how Visnostics can be applied in many more areas of your life beyond sales and marketing.

Politicians, teachers, and police officers are just a few examples of readers that are leveraging Visnostics to enjoy amazing results in their respective careers.

"This is a a great read--thought-provoking, engaging and super practical. It really gets to the heart of what great salespeople do naturally, but many average performers and newer reps struggle with: the ability to create a conversation that leads TO their solution, rather than WITH their solution. I'd highly recommend Kimberlee Slavik's terrific book to anybody looking to take their selling approach to the next level."

-Matthew Dixon, coauthor of The Challenger Sale, The Challenger Customer and The Effortless Experience

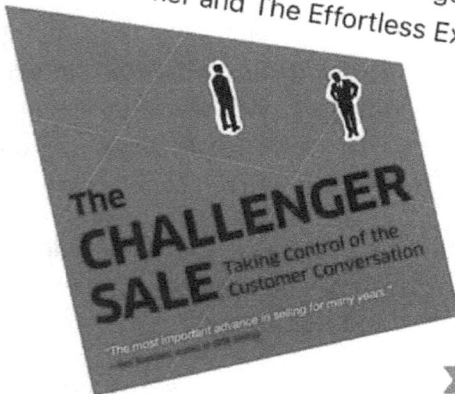

The CHALLENGER SALE Taking Control of the Customer Conversation

"The most important advance in selling for many years."

PIC·COLLAGE

**Jennifer, Sales Channel Marketing & Sales Executive for a Fortune 500 Company (Top 60 with $28 Billion in annual revenue)**

*"With Kim's help we have been able to shift our focus from educating the customer about a specific product to identifying gaps in a customers desired end state and focus our attention on their needs versus our speeds & feeds. The Visnostic Statement method is a powerful tool to get your customers excited about the benefits without ever mentioning the products and services. It's ingenious – easy for sellers as they are simply getting to know their customer better and easy for customers because we are not asking them to make the connections between our offerings and their environment."*

*"As I read 'Visnostic Selling' a light bulb went off in my head; we had been doing it all wrong. No wonder the message wasn't resonating with customers, we were starting with meeting 3. By working with Kim to translate our "Meeting 3" marketing presentation into Visnostics Statements suitable for a first meeting with the customer, we are able to "diagnose" the customer and cater subsequent presentations to their specific needs (that we learn through the visnostic statement scoring). It's brilliant! We've turned a first meeting monologue into an engaging dialogue. Sellers love it. Customers love it. We are making it EASY and engaging for everyone. Thank you Kim! "*

**David Wiener, Senior Sales Leader**

*"During my selling career of 50 years, I read all the sales books and even taught some. I believe the perceived needs of the customer and the apparent solutions to these needs have always controlled the relationship between seller and buyer. This, the weakest point in the sales cycle has never been fully addressed until now.*

*For the last ten years, Kim Slavik has worked on a method for establishing the real customer needs and their priorities. She has also created an easily understood way of establishing and presenting these needs and priorities.*

*Visualization Diagnostic Statements will change the way selling is performed. It is a win-win for buyer and seller. I am honored to have worked with Kim and illustrated her book."*

## Sherry Hall, Award-Winning Author, and Educator

*"While Kim's work most certainly has the potential to be life-changing for salespeople, it also holds implications beyond the world of business. As an educator, I have seen first-hand the power of visualization. I believe Kim's groundbreaking book can create positive change across multiple settings."*

## Phil White former Sales VP, Computer Associates

*"A refreshing common-sense approach of engaging customers and prospects from their perspective. A must read for any modern-day sales organization."*

## James "Jim" Hester, Solution Architect, Pre and Post-Sales Support

*"As a pre-sales solution architect with decades of industry experience, I've noticed certain characteristics that make sales teams more successful than others. A successful sales team must listen more than they speak and absorb everything they see and hear. Although you might think I'm spelling out "Solution Selling," after reading Kim's innovative book you will find that products coupled together do not yield a solution and customers know it. Customers want to differentiate their products and services to their customers but before they can their*

*vendors and partners must listen, prioritize, and gain acceptance of future directions. It is too often assumed that we (as salespeople) truly understand the customer's business almost without any interaction; after all we have a solution for everything. Building and interpreting Visnostic Statements will accelerate a longer, more valued relationship with your customers putting you in the "trusted advisor" driver's seat."*

**Omar Barraza, Marketing Expert, Founder of PlanStartGrow™, and creator of Almost Free Marketing™**

*"Kim's book is the most effective manifesto for revealing the intrinsic value of genuinely understanding a person's professional and personal needs, wants, and expectations. And while her book is destined to become a 'best seller' among resourceful sales professionals, I think it is a 'must read' for anyone in marketing interested in finding new ways to communicate more precisely, accurately, and effectively with past, present and future customers and clients. That's why we now incorporate the principles of Kim's innovative creation when introducing Almost Free Marketing™ and advise our clients to leverage Visnostic Statements too."*

**Pamela Luke, MBA, Sales and Marketing Professional**

*"This powerful book is chock-full of brilliant non-conventional sales and marketing advice on so many levels. One point of value applicable to many industries is the marketing team may never be in a position to purchase the product their company manufactures. Yet, they are required to produce material that will capture the market. This requires a combination of ingenuity and great salesmanship to clinch the deal. Kim takes the reader seamlessly through the steps needed to make the "sell"*

*genuine in order to win while offering positive and engaging motivation."*

## Commander & Lieutenant
## Senior Buyers for the Police Department

*"Personally, having no distinct sales background in marketing or technology, a company recently came in to present their offering of an internet platform they built to show how it could improve work in my field, as I represented a local municipality. I was interested in the concept and eager to see if I thought their product could improve our data collection, as were fifteen other decision makers sitting in the room. Five minutes after they started their PowerPoint presentation I thought to myself "I'm not engaged in this. I do not see why it is important to have this". Ten minutes later looking around the room multiple others had begun checking their phones or otherwise checking out. I had recently read a draft of Kim's book and had multiple conversations with her on Visnostic Statements and the benefits of engaging listeners (clients) in visualization and true feedback. As a consumer or customer, I feel I have a better understanding of what to expect from a product or sales meeting and if the person who says they can provide it, really understands my needs and how their product can fulfill them.*

*I wish this company had read this book or spoken with Kim on truthfully and honestly engaging with the client or end user to prepare their presentation. The presenter did have a valid product they were trying to bring to the market but most likely could have improved market buy in thousands of times faster and more successfully if they had the knowledge this author or her methods bring to the table. "*

## Bridget Cogley, Tableau Zen Master & Visualization Expert

*"We can automate so much. What we can't automate is the human connection, the relationships we build and the novel - and very human - solutions we improvise. Kimberlee understands this, humanizing data and using it to find success in a manner that proves itself time and time again. So, use it to change sales, but use it elsewhere too. Where do you need to build connection and convince others?*

*Visnostic Selling gets to the heart of what clients want - not just what businesses want to throw at them. It lets prospects share their values, deepest dreams, and hopes, so that you - a fellow human - can bond and see a shared path in a way that no automation can provide. You know the potential solution and path your business can provide. What are often missing are the unique gaps clients see, fear, and want to correct. Kimberlee provides a system that's human-centric, allowing us to bypass jargon that's cluttered the path to understanding to get to the root of what clients need. It builds success in a way that's transformational, sustainable, and wildly successful.*

*Use this book to bond and to transform the process so the client shines, you support them on their path, and trust becomes the norm. Expand by letting this process become a longitudinal benchmark, allowing you to return, re-prioritize, and reach new heights with clients. Intuition and data-driven decision-making can work together."*

**Carolynn Boss, Senior Vice President of Sales and Business Development**

*"Having been in Sales more than half of my career, I wish that someone had shared this unique way of approaching a client before. I've been successful in my career but I could have done so much more. So many times, I was forced to*

*use the Company presentation that spent 30-60 minutes bragging about the size and importance of the company I was working for and then went into deep heavy-duty product descriptions that could literally put a client to sleep. Visualization Diagnostic Statements allows the client to be able to understand the benefits he would derive from your technology, understand how it will help his company (and even his career progression when he makes a great decision), while creating an almost automatic sponsor for you while doing it. Sometimes we just need to dare to be different. I find myself looking for the Visualization Diagnostic Statements that should be used for every sales conversation now."*

### Kelly, Account Representative, Ad Agency ($697 Million in annual revenue)

*"The concept of Visnostic Statements has truly revolutionized the way I help my clients develop messaging for their brand. Kim's workshop encouraged my clients to recognize the importance of adopting a customer-centric strategy, which will help their brand resonate with prospective customers and ultimately increase sales of their products."*

### Harrison, Regional Sales Manager for Fortune 100 Company

*"Kim's Visualization Diagnostic Statements will give my team of new sellers a scientific method for how to create content & communicate their company's value to customers. The power in Kim's methodology for my team comes from its simplicity, relatability & ease of deployment in their day-to-day.*

*As a management tool it helps to show where each reps' strengths & weaknesses are so I can continue to develop my people as effectively as possible. Thanks to Kim, my team &*

*I will be more confident in communicating our value to customers."*

**Lynda Stokes, Politician and Former Mayor of Reno, TX**
*"Kimberlee Slavik has done a masterful job in explaining the art of communication/sales through neuroscience.*

*Reading her book is as easy as having coffee with a friend. The stories in this book and the Individual exercises help us to better understand our own thought process in order to communicate with others. As a politician I know we have just a few seconds to grab someone's attention. Kim's book will help you break through the walls we all build. In the business world I am constantly challenged to put myself out there as a product to others. This book is giving me insight and tools to build a vision and the ability to develop visions in others. Therefore, better fulfilling their needs. Putting this into play can pull somebody from the bottom of the barrel and put him or her at the top of the mountain.*

KIMBERLEE SLAVIK

14

# INTRODUCTION
## The Science of VISNOSTICS
## WHY/HOW/WHAT

## WHY you want to read this book

Once upon a time, there was a mother and daughter. One gorgeous afternoon, these lovely women were carrying on a family tradition of cooking a prize-winning roast. The recipe was a closely guarded secret and had been in their family for decades. However, the recipe was extremely precise. The roast had to be an exact weight, the spices had to be carefully measured, the meat had to marinate for a specific amount of time, and even the weather had to be just right for the oven to work its magic.

One day as the mother was teaching all the secrets to the daughter, the roast was properly prepared and it was ready to be put into the pan. Suddenly, the mother pulled out a cutting board and cut the end of the roast off. The daughter was confused and asked the mother why she did that. The mother scratched her head and said, "I honestly don't know. This is how my mother taught me to do it. Let me call her and ask."

The mother called the matriarch and described how perfectly the roast preparation had gone and then asked for the reason they cut off the end of the roast before cooking. The elder mother burst out laughing and said, "Well Honey, I don't know why YOU did it but my pan was too small!"

I absolutely love this story because we have all been guilty of this behavior in some form or fashion during our lives. We tend to do things because it was the way they were always done.

Every once in a while, we will stop and ponder why we do it and if it can be done differently.

If I could summarize this book, this is it. You are about to learn how to do something VERY unique but there is powerful science behind why it works and why you should have been doing it this way your entire life!

In fact, you are about to embark on a journey that will change everything you thought you knew about marketing and sales. Once you have finished this book, you will be armed with powerful knowledge and insight that will inspire you to do things very differently from the way you do them today.

If this book accomplishes what is intended, you will want to review and enhance your current messaging. Visnostics will make your message much more meaningful, impactful, and memorable to your audience.

It will also change the way you purchase things because your expectations will change with how you view a sales process. As a Buyer, you will ask better questions during the purchasing and exploration process.

Your message will be reconstructed to inspire your audience. You will transform your presentations with fewer words and better visuals to ensure your audience remembers your message. They will want to engage with you and share important strengths and weaknesses with you. You will be amazed as your audience becomes enthusiastic about what you have to offer them and their company.

You will NOT be asking questions. You will be making a statement that triggers visualization. And visualization often triggers emotions. The result will be that your audience will give you more information than typically given after a question. And they will ENJOY this new approach!

## People don't just buy from people they like; they buy because they become emotional about the potential solutions and the people from whom they buy.

You will experience for yourself how one simple word can trigger many different emotions and visualizations. Knowing and seeing this will help you ensure you validate your audiences' interpretations of your words. You will become aware of how our brains avoid work and how this avoidance keeps sales and clients out of sync with one another. However, you will also learn how to ensure this isn't a problem in the future.

You will learn the importance of translating your offerings into a language and delivery to which your clients can relate. You will see how this translation step strengthens your relationship with your clients because they will be grateful that you will take this translation burden off their shoulders. You will learn how to take data from your clients and translate that data into valuable information that they can use to sell you and your capabilities internally. You will learn how to create your own tools that will aid in translating pains, weaknesses, challenges, and strengths into an insightful and powerful deliverable for your client. Subsequently, you will change your life, your clients' lives, and the lives of the people around you with this new knowledge and skill!

**You will change your life,
your clients' lives,
and the lives of
the people around you
with this new knowledge and skill!**

-----------------

**WHY & HOW this book is written**

RUSSIAN NESTING DOLLS

Simon Sinek's book *Start With Why* is one of the most-watched Ted Talks of all time with millions of views, and dozens of spin-offs. Sinek created a drawing of three circles with "Why" being the middle starting point. He explains that most companies go right into WHAT they do but they should really start by explaining, "WHY they do what they do." A company should begin each presentation with the purpose and motivation behind what they believe.

The second outer circle should address their process and explain the specific actions they take to support the "WHY." This second step answers HOW they will do what they do.

Finally, the outer most circle and third step should explain WHAT they do. This is when the result of the WHY is explained. Simon Sinek refers to these three steps as "The Golden Circles."

However, when the artist of this book saw the circles, he envisioned that those circles were an aerial view of a Russian Nesting Doll.

For those who don't know what that is, it is a small doll that fits inside a medium doll, that fits inside a large doll. Because visualizations are a critical part of neuroscience, this graphic should help you remember the order in which this thought process flows: Why, How, and What.

I will attempt to follow Simon Sinek's thought process and this Introduction will explain **WHY** I am writing this book, **WHY** you will want to read it, **HOW** you can maximize your benefits and retention of the content, **HOW** you will execute, and **WHAT** you can do to immediately increase your income.

While this is intended to be a stand-alone reference guide, some prerequisite work will help you be much more passionate about what you are about to learn. To truly appreciate and comprehend the content, it will be incredibly helpful for you to understand the basics of Sinek's *Start With Why* because it is full of fundamental details about how the brain works chemically.

After you finish that research, look into *The Challenger Sale* by Matthew Dixon and Brent Adamson, which does an incredible job of explaining why most salespeople never get that important second meeting. It also teaches how to bring true value during your client meetings, which will guarantee that next step in the sales cycle.

## Clients want you to paint a vision of how their lives and companies could be better in the future with your help.

It also does a fantastic job explaining why relationship selling (alone) is not as impactful as previously taught. It explains how to address that so it is actually the most impactful sales approach when combined with the Challenger style.

Finally, please read *What Great Salespeople Do* by Michael Bosworth and Ben Zoldan. It basically explains why *The Bible* is the best-selling book of all times; it is full of stories, and our brains LOVE stories! It teaches how to craft your stories to maximize the impact on your audience. Bosworth's book made so many light bulbs go off in my head that it was blinding.

It felt amazing when I finally realized that my success wasn't just dumb luck or good timing! I had been discounting my abilities for years. Once I understood WHY this worked, I became eager to get BETTER at what I was doing!

**I finally understood the science
behind some of the strange things
I had to do to get my clients
to understand how
I was going to help them.**

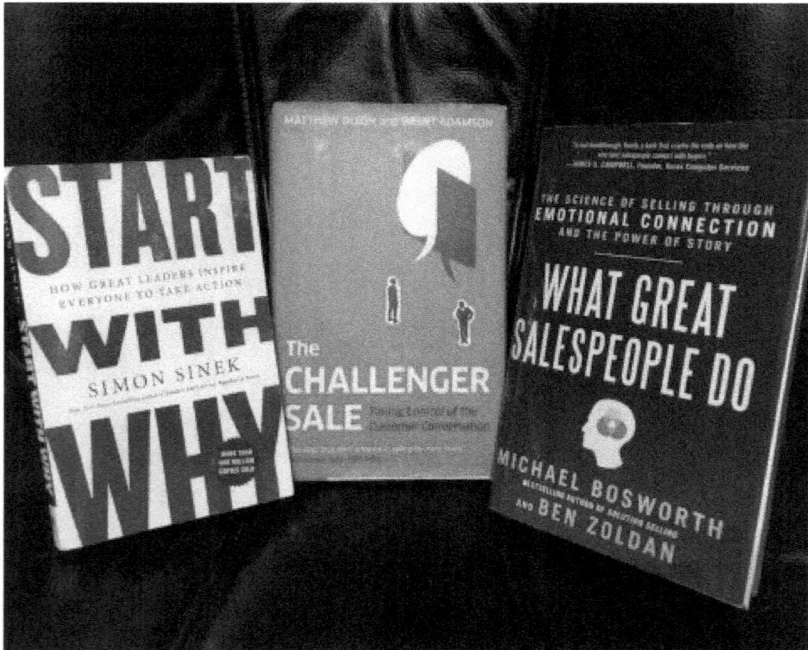

All three of these recommended books are incredible reading by themselves. However, when you combine and execute all three principles, you will harness the most powerful communication approach you have ever seen.

**You must help your audience visualize
how their life could be better
in the future
with your help.**

---

# The Science of Visnostics

Neuroscience is not just beneficial during a sales process; it is also useful in all the relationships in your life. But the value I want to provide to each reader is a detailed description of specific ways you can take the science described, convert what marketing has already created for you, and go deliver the message in a way that your clients want and need you to deliver it!

Basic sales training will teach you to avoid closed-ended questions but sales training never explains WHY. The chemistry in your brain reacts very differently when asked a question requiring a yes or no answer than when it is asked a question that forces a visualization to occur. An example would be:

### Closed-Ended Question – *'Is your car blue?'*
A non-emotional cognitive/cerebral response is triggered.

### Visualization Question – *'What color is your car?'*
A visualization is triggered as they see their car in their thoughts, which will cause a much more emotional response.

Rapport is established during emotional responses, not cerebral ones. It is much easier to resist any decision making when emotions are not engaged.

Did you know that the second question momentarily hijacked your thought process and focused it entirely on your car? This is an automatic response. To see this in action, be sure and do the first exercise. As you read this book, it's designed to help build your own confidence and belief in the power of the science behind Visnostics. This is why the exercises exist.

A closed-ended question requires a cerebral response and a visualization question requires a more emotional response. As sales or marketing professionals, we have been taught that people make emotional decisions much easier than a cerebral one. Emotions create a sense of urgency and a cerebral one can take you down a lengthy sales cycle resulting in the dreaded analysis paralysis.

I will review fundamental principles that you probably already know. However, what is very different with Visnostics is you will learn how to trigger powerful chemicals in the brain that will bond you with your audience like nothing you have ever experienced in the past!

**When done correctly, you won't be asking a question; you will be making a statement.**

**Visnostic Statements force the brain to work harder to respond. This process hijacks the brain and becomes one of the most powerful and profound emotional interactions you can have with another human being during a sales process.**

I've worked with several Neuroscientists to ensure accuracy with this content and I have been told my books simplify a very complex subject so everybody can understand it.

While many sales training programs focus on the cognitive and emotional aspects of the selling process, Visnostics have brought the power of the meta-cognitive to the world of sales training.

What is meta-cognitive? Metacognition refers to our awareness of and ability to regulate our own thinking. Metacognition might be the self-awareness you have around memorization. When you acknowledge that you have difficulty remembering people's names in social situations, you are engaging your metacognitive understanding of yourself.

Now imagine triggering the metacognitive awareness in your clients! Instead of relying on them to translate your features and functions into how they will benefit, you will guide them through the translation process!

I know that makes very little sense to you right now but as you go through the first few chapters of this book, you will comprehend the power of Visualization Diagnostic STATEMENTS versus questions.

By using Visnostic Statements, you will be able to bring the client's wants and wishes to the surface thus avoiding miscommunication. Furthermore, you will now have the power to get the client emotionally engaged within those critical first few seconds!

While this chapter was being written, I was a guest on a very popular sales podcast. First of all, I loved the interview and was honored to be his guest. But I was mortified when I saw that he named the podcast something like *"Use this type of QUESTION to win deals!"* **VISNOSTIC STATEMENTS ARE NOT QUESTIONS!!!!!** As I listened to the recording, I realized that he actually edited out all of my comments about how questions are not effective. So it was no surprise that his commentary after my interview focused on selling his training around questioning!

Despite what you may have been taught, questioning isn't the Holy Grail to understanding client needs.

Consultative Selling was all the rage in the early 2000's and I took about a dozen different classes on how to ask questions to qualify my clients' needs. However, when I was attempting to execute the questioning principles, I could FEEL my clients getting annoyed.  Think about this – when you are on the phone with a support person, they will usually ask you to take a short survey after the call. Do you actually take the time to do them? I worked for a Customer Experience Company and I can tell you that the surveys are rarely done.

Have you ever walked through a mall and someone with a clipboard tried to get you to take a quick survey? Are you excited to do it? Personally, I want to chew a body part off to escape. This desire to resist surveys is also triggered when we blast our clients with a barrage of questions.

Visnostics will teach you about the natural instincts we all have around "Fight or Flight." Questioning will absolutely trigger these resistance responses. Visnostic Statements are a better way to get the answers you need without actually asking questions!! And your clients will appreciate this new approach.

What if you could learn a communication style that would release serotonin in your client's brain versus the Fight or Flight response as you spoke?

This is what Wikipedia says about serotonin - *As a neurotransmitter, serotonin helps to relay messages from one area of the brain to another. ... This includes brain cells related to mood, sexual desire and function, appetite, sleep, memory and learning, temperature regulation, and some social behavior.*

The power in triggering serotonin in your clients' brains is very similar to Pavlov's Dog. Just as Pavlov conditioned a dog to salivate every time he rang a bell; your clients will relate good feelings when they think of YOU.

## Triggering the release of serotonin is an incredible way to establish respect, rapport, and credibility instantly!

---

# WHY this book has more graphics and fewer words than most business books

Look closely at this graphic. Did you know that our attention spans are getting shorter at an alarming rate?

In 2000, you had twelve seconds to grab the attention of your audience. In 2015, you only had eight seconds! To put that into perspective, a goldfish has a nine-second attention span. That means that a goldfish will pay attention longer than a human today!

The same year this book was published, the first class of "Generation Z" entered the workforce. Studies have shown that this generation has a THREE-SECOND attention span! That means that your first three words of your message MUST appeal to the reader instantly.

I have worked with enough salespeople to tell you that I highly suspect the typical salesperson has an even lower attention span than a typical human!

With that in mind, the average business book has over 70,000 words and few graphics, each of my books will have less than 35,000 words and several dozen graphics. **Why** am I doing that? Because I want every reader to actually finish reading the entire contents in one sitting AND the pictures will help readers remember the content!

In addition to these books with just 35,000 words and less than 200 pages, I will also be co-writing Visnostic "Special Editions" with experts in specific fields. These books will be about half the size because the focus will be on specific industries.

The goal is that readers will execute and receive an immediate value on a topic very important to them. Once they see the power of Visnostics, they will want to read the complete book so they can become more advanced in these very powerful new skills.

I once read that a study was conducted on college students attending the same class, learning from the same books, the same instructor, and taking the same tests.  However, one group did better than the other.  The only difference was that one group attended classes Monday, Wednesday, and Friday for one hour each day.  The other group attended Tuesday and Thursday for one hour and thirty minutes each day.  The study concluded that the shorter the instruction, the better the retention. I'm not sure if this is true or not, but it's another data point to support my strategy of using fewer words by leveraging more visuals.

*"You are Who You Are, Because of Where You Were, When"* is one of my all-time favorite quotes by Dr. Morris Massey. I recommend that you familiarize yourself with this concept. Entire books have been written on this subject so we won't be able to spend much time dissecting it. However, understanding this concept will enhance your ability to have empathy for your audience. If you understand the basic concept and the importance of adapting to your audience, you will be even better at learning this new communication process. Here is a URL to help you quickly grasp the primary points of this theory – It is a video from the '80s but if you listen closely, you will realize why it's age makes the message even more impactful.

https://www.youtube.com/watch?v=_aY163kwlW4

From my perspective, I love to learn and I love to try new things. Therefore, throughout my career, I embraced the latest sales training that came out. While each book or training course was incredible, and I always learned something new from each one, I also scratched my head in bewilderment. Don't writers know that most salespeople have an incredibly short attention span? Why are books so long? And why are they full of so much 'filler'? When am I supposed to have time to read all these books? Do publishers demand a certain number of pages or words to legitimize the content?

Well, here is the reality of MY world as an eager reader and student – I would get a new book, enthusiastically start reading and by about the fifth chapter, life disrupted my reading and I had to put down the book. A few days or even weeks later, when I got back to the book, I would feel the need to scan the first chapters again to get my head back in the game.

I have dozens of business books in my office and even more audiobooks on various devices. I bet I have read or listened to the first five chapters dozens of times. Sadly, I usually finished them only once! I'm embarrassed to admit this, but I am pretty sure that I have a couple of fantastic books that I never even finished! So why do that to someone else?

The goal is that with less than 35,000 words, you will read each of my books in one sitting; this should increase the probability that you take your excitement and execute while it is fresh in your memory.

In fact, I plan on having you execute in Chapter ONE so not only will you see first-hand the power of neuroscience, you will have the confidence to do it TODAY! I also want you to believe in what you are reading. The exercises are critical so you can see these concepts work instantly. As each point is proven to you, you will become more passionate about leveraging these new skills immediately.

# WHY exercises will help you learn and retain and execute more effectively

Most of you have probably seen versions of this graphic throughout your career. Which means you all should know that your ability to retain what you learn is maximized when you 'teach' the materials. Therefore, as you read, you will notice multiple exercises that are intended to simulate a teaching scenario that will enhance your comprehension.

Unfortunately, per neuroscience and human nature, you will be tempted to skip the exercises. Even though doing the exercises with other people will increase your ability to remember and comprehend the content, you will convince yourself that you are special and don't need this enhancement for adequate learning. Fight this urge!

Why waste your time reading this book if you only retain 10% of what you read? Doing each exercise will ensure you not only read, but also, hear, see, discuss, experience, and teach. By retaining 95% of what is in the book, you will not waste your valuable time reading a book that you won't remember and you will be more prepared to actually execute these powerful new skillsets!

## WHY Graphics are powerful

I also want to explain **why** there is a need for so many graphics. As I shared a draft of this book, I was thrilled how many people gave feedback by referring to the graphics associated with the content. Graphics help the reader retain the information!

Take a look at your current presentations and websites. Do you have more words than pictures? Do your graphics compliment your words? If not, this needs to change immediately. When graphics and words don't complement each other, it confuses the audience. This confusion will cause them to disengage.

Recently I read an article on LinkedIn by Inc. called **"7 Presentation Ideas That Work for Any Topic."** https://www.inc.com/carmine-gallo/7-presentation-ideas-that-work-for-any-topic.html

First of all, I agree with every single word in this article, but I questioned the author as I read it because it instructed the reader to use more pictures than words. Yet there were no pictures. It said to avoid bullets but each point was numbered AND there were bullets. In my opinion, a bullet and a number are the same things. This made the article seem somewhat hypocritical to me and it is important that I don't do that to my readers.

My point here is that I am going to teach you how to do things and I am going to "lead by example" as much as possible. In fact, if you catch me falling short, be sure to communicate your observations with me so I can fix it in future releases! It is so easy to read HOW to do something, but it is a much bigger challenge to go out there and actually execute what you learned!

## How can an author legitimize the content if the advice is not followed during the instruction?

Therefore, you will notice that almost every page will have at least one photo or graphic highlighting a point made in the content. This serves multiple purposes. I want you to remember the content but I also want you to find what you are looking for when you need to go back and reference, re-read, or find something.

## These points are not intended to instruct you how I am writing a book; they are intended to inspire you to follow this same logic when creating communications with your clients.

I have so many random facts in my head, yet I am challenged to remember who said it or from what book it came. My goal is that while you visualize the artwork, you will remember the content, and be able to quickly reference what you need in the future.

Furthermore, as I travel, teach, and present this methodology, the graphics will replace most of the words and become the focal point of my presentations to improve the retention of the content.

## Visualization is a major part of the power of neuroscience.

You will also notice repetition as you read. Studies have uncovered that the mind has to absorb information multiple times and multiple ways to comprehend and retain the concept. So if you find yourself reading something familiar yet a little different, this has been done intentionally to help you retain the content.

## The importance of two-way communications

As you look at these two drawings, imagine you are one of the characters in each scene. Which drawing seems to represent the most pleasant form of communication? Do you prefer to be in listen mode or do you prefer to be engaged in the communication process?

Pause as you look at these two scenes and dissect why you chose one over the other. Why is two-way communication scenario so much more attractive than a one-way communication scenario? Why do some people struggle with reading? Which scene is most like reading a book? Isn't reading similar to listening mode? Why do we need classrooms if we can just read books and learn the content?

One of the Visnostic Readers wrote me an told me about a recent graduation commencement speech and he asked his nephew what he thought of the speaker. The response was that the speech was long and boring. Isn't that what we each remember about our own graduations? Can you recall anything that was said? Can you recall the topic? Do you realize it was a one-way-communication? It was long, painful, boring, and unmemorable. Do we really want this same effect on our clients? I know I don't want it to happen to my readers!

Have you ever read an interactive book? I don't think I have! I am sure they exist but they are most certainly in short supply. This is interesting because we are taught in neuroscience that one-way communications are not stimulating and they are unnatural.

Therefore, I will be asking you to do some exercises and to email me your stories. This may seem like a silly thing to do, but it will help you retain what you learned. It will also help you to visualize the emotions you just witnessed. It will be a good experience for you so you will be prepared to convert these approaches to your work life. The ultimate goal is that you will increase your pipeline immediately.

**How much you get out of this book is up to you and is dependent upon how well you follow these instructions.**

# WHAT are Visualization Diagnostic Statements™?

NOTE - Also referred to as a VDS, Diagnostic Statement, or Visnostic in this book.

Visnostic Statements and Visualization Diagnostic Statements are trademarked terms created by Kimberlee Slavik, CEO of DynaExec. They are statements that require a response from an audience. They stimulate emotional responses inspiring your audience to maximize their interest in your message. Visualization Diagnostic Statement is the scientific term. However, readers may want to refer to it by a term more in alignment with their specific business and client base.

# The statements typically <u>translate</u> features and functions into something more meaningful to the audience.

A Visnostic Statement often originates as an ineffective, generic, one-way **self-focused** message that has been converted into a meaningful two-way engaging statement that is **audience-focused**. Existing presentations, brochures, case studies, and other marketing materials are often reworded to become Visnostic Statements.

A Visnostic Statement is also a qualification tool that will help you assess your audience. As you go through the statements, if your participant isn't responding or is struggling with responding, chances are high that you aren't in front of the right participant.

A Visnostic Statement is also an effective way to determine if sales and marketing currently have the right messaging. If creating these statements feels effortless, the current messaging is strong. When these statements are difficult to create, the content doesn't contain what the clients need and want to know.

Visnostic Statements will change the way you think. For example, I was helping a reader improve his resume and I commented that there were no results mentioned. He argued that his job didn't produce any results from his efforts. I challenged him to go research some statistics. This young man was in a support role and his relationship with the client was after a sale was completed. He enthusiastically called me back a few days later to tell me that the account he helped, paid the company over 1.5 million dollars annually. He concluded that if he didn't do a good job providing support, the company would lose that revenue stream. He now realizes his value to the company thanks to the research needed to develop Visnostic Statements.

## The Importance of A Diagnostic Approach
## Cause versus Symptom

I recently participated in a group interview for a sales leadership role. Several people described things they saw as broken in the sales organization and they asked me how I would fix these problems. The complaints ranged from sales were down to morale was low. My response to them was that they were describing a symptom and asking me how to eliminate the pain before I understood the cause of that pain. For my response, I used the analogy of a headache and how a physician would handle a patient with the same dilemma.

Prescribing a painkiller to help the headache go away will not address the cause of the pain; it will only temporarily mask the symptom. I continued by explaining that multiple things could cause a headache such as allergies, caffeine withdrawal, vision problems, medications, a hangover, hormones, a brain tumor, just to name a few. Yet each cause of these pains must be treated very differently to eliminate the SOURCE of the pain.

Just as a good doctor will dig deeper and run tests to determine the cause of the pain, a good salesperson or sales leader should also investigate to ensure he or she is addressing the correct cause of the issues. For example, I typically interview people, review reports, analyze the competitive marketplace, and examine existing business tools in order to uncover the cause of the problem.

Too often enthusiastic and new sales professionals will start attempting to fix the symptom versus taking the necessary extra time to uncover the cause of the issues. This happens with internal pains as well as client pains.

Not until a successful diagnosis of the **cause** of the pain is made, can the appropriate plan of action be executed to eliminate the **source** of the pain.

Visnostic Statements should be constructed to identify your clients' pains and the cause of their pains. It is the responsibility of the sales organization to differentiate pains, challenges, and weaknesses as either causes or symptoms.

Converting typical sales points into this unique format will engage your client and create the desire to share important details that will help properly diagnose the cause and how the client can be helped.

## Why This Is Relevant and Important

If a salesperson is taught a presentation and delivers the presentation on sales calls, do they really understand the client's source of the pain?

Converting marketing content into "Visnostic Statements" is the first step in creating a powerful tool that will help diagnose the most effective areas in which the sales team can help the client. Visnostic Statements will create an environment that will stimulate meaningful and valuable conversations with the client.

## WHAT Buyers Learn

I knew this book would benefit sales professionals, marketing teams, sales leaders, and any other client-facing roles in an organization. I never envisioned that BUYERS would find the content of value. However, as I was having close friends and family review the draft, I received some unexpected feedback from two people with zero sales backgrounds. While they didn't sell for a living, they did have frequent purchasing requirements and were often forced to endure some pretty tough and painful sales presentations.

I was excited to hear that a few weeks after reading a draft, a very important sales presentation was conducted. People that had a vested interest in learning more about the offering attended the meeting. These two people just happened to be in the same presentation and they told me they viewed the salespeople very differently after learning about the concepts around Visnostic Statements.

They explained that they were on opposite sides of the room, texting each other about how horrible the slides were. They were full of words and bullets and had very few graphics that made sense. They looked around the room and observed the entire audience was disengaged and on their various smart devices. The salespeople had lost the interest of the entire room and now my two friends understood why the presentation was not effective!

These two people went on to explain that they are stronger and more educated buyers after reading the draft. They continued explaining that their expectations are higher than they were before reading the book. They also suggested that I reach out to the company that presented to them because they actually want to buy the offering.  However, the salespeople simply didn't build a strong enough case to justify the purchase! This is such terrific insight from Buyers!  Therefore, try and imagine how your clients would react to the content you are reading. What would YOUR clients say about YOUR interaction with them?

## VDS are Universally Effective

Even though my career has been primarily associated with Silicon Valley companies, Visnostic Statements should apply to all sales and marketing scenarios.  For example, if you are a Real Estate Agent and you sell houses based upon the number of bedrooms, bathrooms, square footage, and price, you will sell more if you lead with the real reason clients actually buy homes. One of the greatest Agents I ever worked with told me that she didn't sell homes; she sold dreams.  Creating effective VDS will flush out those dreams.

I'm also working with a paint company that insists their buyers buy on price and relationships.  They believe that all of their Buyers consider paint to be a commodity.  My response to this comment was, **"If your clients view your offerings as a commodity, you are SELLING it as a commodity; VDS will highlight the differentiators that will help change this perspective."**

To summarize this introduction, you now know WHY this book was written, why you should follow the instructions, and why it is formatted in an unusual way. You also now understand HOW to get the most out of what you read, and WHAT the outcome should be for you, your company, and your clients.

# CHAPTER ONE
## Believing is doing
## The Birth of Visualization Diagnostic Statements

I n 2004 I represented a company and a service that I was so passionate about that I invested in the company. I sincerely believed that I had ten-dollar bills for sale for just one dollar.

Think about that! If someone gave you a stack of ten-dollar bills and told you that they would pay you commissions to go sell them for one dollar, wouldn't you call every person you knew? Wouldn't you jump out of bed in the morning and go on sales calls with tremendous enthusiasm? I was setting up at least five meetings each day and I would have done more but I ran out of daylight. I still hold sales records at that company! That was my life for the first decade of my career and I sincerely believed that my customers loved me for educating them on what I was selling.

However, there was this one client that shocked and frustrated me because he didn't seem to see the value I brought to him and his company. This is the story of how Visualization Diagnostic Statements were born.

The first time I presented to him, he fell asleep. HE FELL ASLEEP! Of course, he was embarrassed and set up another meeting. I was actually encouraged during the second meeting because I noticed him taking very vigorous notes. He seemed to be really concentrating and really into what he was writing down. I walked over to him and he was doing his grocery list. HE WAS DOING HIS GROCERY LIST!

I was young and so bewildered that someone wasn't paying attention to me!  After all, I WAS SELLING TEN DOLLAR BILLS FOR JUST ONE DOLLAR! I had lost him for the second time and I was frustrated because I had been working with him for a year. What added to this frustration was that I KNEW he would love me for what I could do for him! How could he not want to pay attention to what I had to say?

I actually stopped the presentation and pleaded with him to tell me what I was doing wrong. He said nothing was wrong. He then stated that he had to be honest with me; he didn't have a budget to buy anything so he was just meeting with me to be nice. (Why do Clients think that wasting our time and disrespecting us as Professionals is being nice?)

At that moment, I knew I had to approach things very differently for him to digest how I could rock his world with my service. He told me that he was sorry that he wasted my time. I thanked him for his honesty and I left but I didn't stop thinking about what he said and what I did NOT say.

One of my personal mottos was "No" means "Try Harder." So I accepted the fact that I was accountable for this failure because I was doing something ineffective and I needed to try harder, or in this case try something different.

I was convinced that my presentation just wasn't keeping his attention. I thought of all the things that I should have said to him while I was there. My software didn't need a budget because the return on investment was extremely high and it was fast.

How could I go back to him and deliver this message differently? How could I get him to listen to me? A third presentation was out of the question.

I don't know how I came up with this idea. I don't think I am that smart so it must have been some type of divine intervention. I took my slide deck and for the first time, I really dissected what each bullet said. Why wasn't this working? It was the same deck I used to sell everybody else so why didn't this guy get excited too?

I tried to put myself in his shoes and read my presentation through his eyes. I never really looked at my messaging through my clients' eyes. I always viewed my presentation as MY story and MY COMPANY's story.

I suddenly realized that my client has his own story and his own problems. He didn't care about my company story! I also noticed for the first time that each bullet sounded so generic. I sounded like each of my competitors. I sounded like I could have been selling anything.

I then reviewed our other marketing tools such as brochures, web pages, advertisements, infographics, and anything else I could find that explained what we did for our clients. For the first time, I found myself looking for RESULTS and I realized that they were extremely difficult to find in our current "sales tools!"

I reworded each marketing point. Instead of approaching the communication with "this is what WE can do for you," I changed the wording to be a statement that HE would make.

When I first created these statements, I called them "Challenge Statements." However, when I started to document my experiences, I researched that term. I discovered that the definitions and descriptions were an established legal term. This did not align with what I was doing. I worried that referring to these phrases as Challenge Statements would cause too much confusion.

So I changed the term to "Diagnostic Statements" but quickly discovered this was also an established term used in nursing.

It is because of these past name changes that, "Visualization Diagnostic Statements" has been trademarked. While this current term better describes the science behind what is accomplished, unfortunately, it was a mouthful and difficult to say. Therefore, by combining Visualization and Diagnostics, the word, Visnostics was born and trademarked!

I am explaining this because in a few pages, you will see a copy of the original document. I want to avoid any confusion the different terms may cause the readers. Challenge Statements, Visnostic Statements, Diagnostic Statements, Visualization Diagnostic Statements, and VDS are the same thing. Both the name and the process have evolved throughout the years.

I then made four columns in a Word document. I labeled these columns "Would like to say this," "Say this today," "NA, Not important, or do not know" and "Challenge Statement."

Next, I took each presentation bullet describing the features/functions/benefits of what I was selling and made each bullet a line item. But first I translated them from "We can do this..." into "I can do this..." These became the first "Challenge Statements."

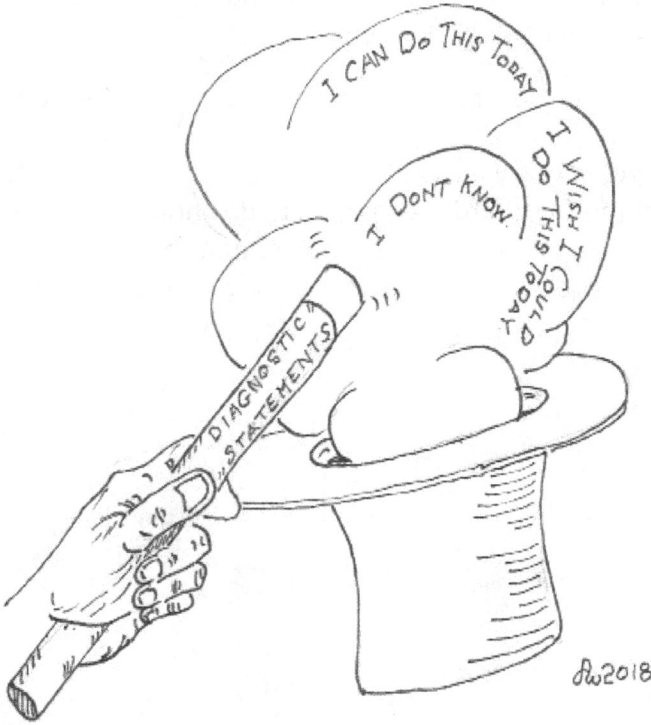

Once this new document was completed, I called the client back and asked him to go to lunch with me. At first, he resisted and reminded me that he didn't have a budget and wasn't going to buy from me. I reassured him that I heard that message loud and clear in our meeting, but I really needed a favor. I promised not to try selling him anything. I just needed his advice on how I could do things better in the future.

I explained that I had created a new tool that I wanted to share and listen to his valuable feedback. Once he knew I wasn't trying to sell him, he agreed to lunch. I suspect there may even be a chapter in neuroscience about our eagerness to respond when someone needs our help.

I could actually feel his defensive walls come crashing down. I'm not sure if it was the offer of a free lunch, the promise that I wasn't going to try and sell him again, or that I needed his help that got me that third meeting. But I do know that his "Fight or Flight" instinct had been disengaged and this was a huge step in correcting what had gone wrong during the first two meetings.

Two Way Communication

 flw 2018

Once we were at lunch and had our food, I pushed my plate aside. I apologized to him for trying to force a presentation. I explained that this time I had a different approach that didn't require a projector, conference room, or even a laptop.

All I had was a piece of paper with printing on one side. I told him that I was going to make a statement and with each statement, I would need him to respond with one of three responses. "I can do this today," "I wish I could do this today," or "I don't know, not important, not applicable."

NOTE: After reading this book, Bosworth began referring to these client responses as "AFFIRMATIONS" and he actually wrote about these affirmations in the Foreword. However, be careful not to confuse the client affirmations with the actual statements. A statement is always a statement even after the client responds, but not all client responses will be affirmations. For example, if a client responds to the statement, "not important" or "not applicable," the client response is NOT an affirmation. However, the statement is still a statement. This is an important principle to understand while reading this book.

He agreed and I started with the first line. "Restore is a simple and visual process." His eyes immediately looked up and to the left; I was stunned. I had been taught that salespeople should look for this body language because it meant that the audience was envisioning something that would get them emotionally engaged in the conversation.

To my surprise, not only did he say he WISHED he could do that today, he elaborated on how they did it today and how long it took and how painful it was. He even told me a story about how the CEO had accidentally deleted an email. The CEO frantically called the IT department and explained that this was an emergency and he needed them to restore that email immediately.

However, it took over twenty-four hours to find the backup of the deleted email and restore it. In fact, someone had actually been terminated because it took so long to restore. He explained that the inability of the IT Department to restore lost data in a timely manner was now extremely visible at the CEO level and the IT department was now considered to be incompetent at the highest level within the company.

Wow! That was some valuable information about the "pain" he was feeling in his current role.

I restored the original document I designed in 2004 so I could include a copy to share here. I did edit it and took out all references to what company this was, the competitors, and specific shared applications names that were needed.

Company Name:
Date: 2004
Because the XYZ solution is very robust, and we have a limited amount of time to demonstrate the software, please take a moment to answer the following questions so our presentation can be customized for you and your company.

1. Attendees

| Name | Title | Function |
|------|-------|----------|
|      |       |          |

2. Specific "Deleted" Concerns – What are THREE "challenges" that you are tasked with or most concerned about?

| Name | Challenge #1 | Challenge #2 | Challenge #3 |
|------|--------------|--------------|--------------|
|      | Compliancy   | No budget    | With (competitors name) today |

3. Please put a check mark next to one of the three options describing your current situation with back-up and restore

| Would LIKE to say this | SAY this TODAY | NA, Not Important or do not know (?) | Challenge Statement |
|---|---|---|---|
| ✓ | | | Restore is a simple and visual process |
| | ✓ | | Quickly and easily find and restore missing files |
| ✓ | | | Avoid wasteful and costly differential back-up jobs |
| ✓ | | | In seconds, scroll back in time to view past server state |
| ✓ | | | Missing files and directories are seen as conspicuous cross-hatched objects and a single click launches the restore job |
| ✓ | | | Reduce hardware costs by exploiting inexpensive serial ATA-devices. |
| | ✓ | | Decrease backup time |
| ✓ | | | Ultra quick restores from disk |
| ✓ | | | Integrate Disk-to-Disk-to-Tape with Synthetic Full Backup to maximize benefits. |
| | | N/A | Backup time shrinks drastically |
| ✓ | | | Only incremental backups are needed. (XYZ performs full back-ups 1x wk) |
| ✓ | | | Reduce network traffic by only sending incremental data over the LAN. |
| ✓ | | | Restore time is optimized since restore is from the synthetic full job on disk/tape. |
| ✓ | | | Potentially run incremental backups forever and synthetic fulls. |
| ✓ | | | Avoid wasteful and costly differential back-up jobs |
| | ✓ | | Create offsite tapes during your regular, nightly backups |
| ✓ | | | Simultaneously write to disk and tape |
| ✓ | | | Save time by not having to re-run backups or having to duplicate tapes during the day. |
| ✓ | | | The ability to backup through a single port created as a secure outbound connection. |
| ✓ | | | No open (inbound) ports are needed for backup |
| | ✓ | | The ability to restart a job from the point of failure |
| | | ? | The ability to pause an active job midstream? |
| | | ? | Failed backup jobs over the LAN can be automatically restarted and pick-up from where they left off and not restart the job over from the beginning |
| | ✓ | | Pause and restart an active job at any time for any reason |
| | | ? | Ability to restore your own data through a web browser |
| | | ? | Personalize XML-based reports |
| ✓ | | | Align costs with SLAs |
| ✓ | | | Vendor appreciates you and treats you as a valued partner |

**Don't bother trying to read it. I just want you to see how unpolished it was.**

Despite being primitive, ugly, and very simplistic, it was so much more effective than my gorgeous, fifty slides, professionally crafted presentation that the company provided to me! How crazy is THAT?!

I know it's impossible to read. I was selling business continuity software. However, no need to spend any time trying to read the details in the "Statement" section because the details are not important. Just know that each statement originally was a bullet in a presentation; this was the same presentation during which this client fell asleep and wrote his grocery list! And yet his reaction to this approach was completely opposite of my professional presentation. Nobody was more surprised than me at this stage of my career!

**The reality is that the client doesn't care about all the cosmetics if you can't get him/her engaged in the content and have an intelligent, two-way dialogue.**

### If the client isn't talking, the salesperson isn't learning how to help the client!

I realize that this sounds so logical and simple. However, all sales professionals know just how difficult it can be to get clients to share information. And now we know WHY – "The Fight or Flight" instinct is a powerful adversary during each sales cycle.

The secret to overcoming this response is to get them emotionally, not just intellectually, engaged.

**Creating effective Visnostic Statements and asking your audience to reflect and respond is the tactical instruction that has been missing from every sales methodology book that I have read.**

This Visnostic process is unique and like nothing you have ever been taught until now.

It's important to understand that this isn't a theory or hypothesis. It is a methodology that I have been utilizing for over ten years and it has worked at multiple companies with different products and services.

It is also an approach that none of my clients have ever seen another salesperson do. It is a universal technique and since nobody is doing it, it will be refreshing to your clients when you approach them with this new communication style. That is until the lessons taught in this book become normal business practices.

This process has evolved but I will help you with the basics first and then I will explain some enhancements that have been added through the years. And as I demonstrated earlier, it doesn't have to be pretty to be effective.

About half-way through the list of my Visnostic Statements, he pushed his plate of food aside and he commented that he assumed my company could do all this or we wouldn't be going through this exercise. I said that was correct. He then asked me why the heck I didn't tell him this before now!

I looked him straight in the eyes and told him that this is the presentation that I gave him TWICE! **He laughed and said none of it even sounded familiar to him!**

## This is when I realized that marketing content relies too heavily on clients' abilities to translate and interpret the actual benefits.

This new way of presenting the same information was allowing me to guide him through the thought process by eliminating the translation requirement. The result was that instead of dumping everything I could do for my client in a presentation and depending on him to translate, I was able to guide him to his own conclusion.

I also noticed that I talked a lot less and the client talked a lot more. In fact, I noticed how passionately the client started opening up to me! This was an incredible thing to witness! I NEVER got this type of reaction during a presentation!

## The client came to his own conclusion versus me telling him what to think. When it is his or her idea, they will become more receptive.

He then asked if I could send him an electronic version of this new document, including his responses, by close of business that same day! I said of course!

I left the meeting and typed it all up, along with some of his commentary, which I had written on the back of this paper. He called me the next day with questions. He confessed that he edited the document and was presenting it to the CEO as his own research with a recommendation to go with us to fix specific problems that would address the restoration delays the CEO had witnessed.

Within a month of this lunch, the deal closed and it made my number for the entire year. This was a client that had no budget and obviously no interest in my presentation because **his mind**

**was on his own problems, not what my company had to say about our company.** Aren't most clients having this same experience when we take their valuable time?

Salespeople talk way too much about their company and what they can do. Companies need their marketing departments to address this immediately! I can honestly say that nobody has ever bought from me because of the stock prices, our acquisitions, or the company strategy. They buy because of the positive way their business will be impacted. I hope as people from both sales and marketing read the Visnostic books, they see their messaging from a completely different perspective so it can be changed!

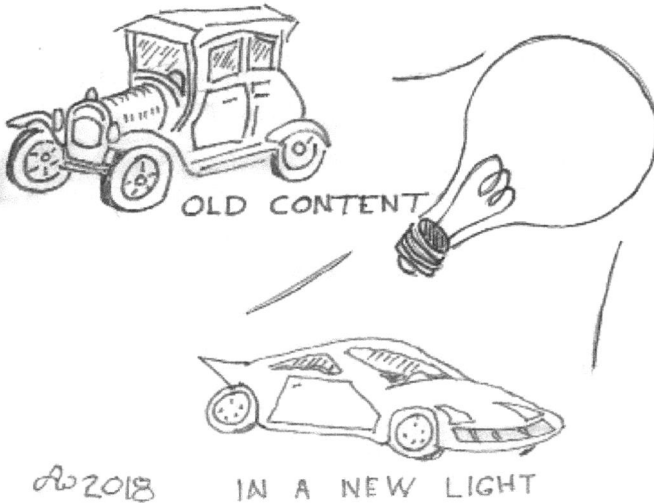

OLD CONTENT

IN A NEW LIGHT

I felt like I had just invented the light bulb with this new approach! "No" means "Try Harder" or in this case, "No" meant that I needed to try something different.

How can you fix something that you didn't realize was broken?

**My content was exactly the same. The only difference was the way in which the content was communicated; It's not WHAT you say, it's HOW you say it!**

**This was when I realized that HOW you articulate your message is more important than the actual content!**

This story happened over 10 years ago and I have successfully used this approach at both big companies and small companies. I was never sure why this worked or what to call it. But as I read Mike Bosworth's most recent book, *What Great Salespeople Do*, I finally understood that this wasn't just dumb luck; there is some heavy-duty science behind it. Today, we call it Neuroscience. And it's powerful because it works!

Since 2004, I have been converting presentation bullets into this format and taking this approach with my clients with huge success. This methodology has even evolved into something more powerful. Today, when a client responds with "I can do or say this today," I now ask him to grade himself with a one through five rating system.

The scoring goes like this; if the client gives himself a one, that means they can do it but they have a lot of room for improvement. If the client scores himself a five, it means that he can do it today and he views it as perfect.

Now that you know the history of Visualization Diagnostic Statements as well as some of its evolution over the past decade, let's review some basic neuroscience that you will soon observe first hand. I am confident that each reader will be amazed to find this part of the book to be enlightening and fun.

## Fun facts about how your brain works

3 CANDLES    3 MICE

3 PEAKS

Aw 2018

## The Power of THREEs

Because this book is focused on the Auto Industry, you HAVE to go watch this GMC commercial about the "Rule of Threes" – https://www.youtube.com/watch?v=SY23zi1u_3U

You are about to have your first experience with executing neuroscience exercises. Some of the exercises will go extremely well while others will have some challenges and may not even work at all. But don't be discouraged.

Activities before and during the learning process will increase your retention of the content. After you read the entire book, go back and retry the exercises to see how much you have improved. It will be a great opportunity to see your progress while you evaluate your understanding of this new approach. It will also build your confidence that you are ready to execute with your clients.

There are so many books out today about neuroscience, which is basically a cool new buzzword for psychology. One of the points I read recently about neuroscience is to engage with your clients as soon as possible, which is why chapter one starts with some executable exercises for the reader.

I also attended a leadership conference for women recently that taught the audience that the male brain prefers to have selections in groups of threes. To prove her point, the speaker showed us advertisements for three different tires. The speaker also told us that men prefer three colors of pants in their wardrobe: black, khaki, and blue. She supported these claims by having the only six men in the audience come on stage and she was correct; they all had on those colors of pants. These two simple new things I learned, helped validate why what I am about to share with you really does work and it works well!

The purpose of this story is to help you understand why I have three exercises for you to do in Chapter One, why you will see other topics in this book developed in sets of three.

And more importantly – **Why Visnostic Statements Have THREE Options For Your Clients To Consider!**

Per the facts mentioned above, at least fifty percent of our population prefers choices in threes or odd numbers. But I actually think the percentage is much higher.

# 3 CANDLES

The points made about men's brains reminded me of a woman's decorating class that taught that we think we want symmetrical settings, but our brain actually prefers things in uneven numbers.

Therefore, it can be concluded that these preferences in groups of threes may apply to women as well as men.

As you conduct Visnostic discussion, you will be tempted to take short cuts or simplify by just offering ONE of the THREE selections but if you do that, you just converted a statement into a question! AND you will be eliminating the POWER OF THREES! Do NOT do that!

You will make your Visnostic STATEMENT (speaking from the Client's perspective) and ask them to select one of three responses:

1. **I can say this today. (If so, score yourself 1-5 with 5 being perfect)**
2. **I WISH I could say this today.**
3. **It's not important, I don't know, or not applicable.**

**Visnostic Discussions are NOT Questions! Questions are risky and can trigger the "Fight or Flight" instinct that we all have.**

People that sell training on how to ask questions will argue this claim so let me give an example to prove my point why questions alone won't help you understand your clients:

Do you get excited and eager when you receive a call from someone asking you to spend just a few minutes as they conduct a survey? Do you eagerly wait after a support call so you can respond to the survey about your satisfaction with the call? If you answer yes, you are an anomaly. For most people, this is an annoyance. We need to know what is in it for US? If you write your statements correctly, your first three words will clearly explain what is in it for your audience.

For more information, please look in the Appendix; you will find additional articles that will support the points I make about Visnostic Statements and why statements are much more impactful than questions. But the reality is that we will never eliminate the need for SOME questions as we interact with others.

# Fight or Flight or Freeze

There are a few fundamental human instincts to keep in mind as you read the following directions. First of all, "fight or flight" is a real thing that haunts salespeople. Humans have a natural instinct to put up walls, become defensive, or flee when someone is trying to sell to them, ask them for money, or persuade them.

You don't believe this? When you see a sales call on your caller ID, do you enthusiastically answer your phone? When you answer the phone and it is a charity or salesperson, do you hang-up on them? Do you interrupt and tell them that you don't have time to talk? What other tactics do you use to avoid listening to them pitch to you? When you walk into a store, and a salesperson asks if they can help you, do you attempt to brush them off by telling them that you are just looking? Your responses were probably very much like the responses you have towards SURVEYS (i.e. QUESTIONS)!

As you read that there will be exercises, do you recall how that made you feel? Even if it occurred in your subconscious, I bet that you already decided and JUSTIFIED why you don't need to do the exercises. Am I right? Humans are complex but we can be incredibly predictable as well.

Because I have been selling my entire career, you would think that I would be more receptive and patient with salespeople. However, I am far from it. I even took the time to add all of my numbers to the United States Do Not Call Registry.

The **Do Not Call Registry** accepts registrations from both cell phones and land lines. To **register** by telephone, **call** 1-888-382-1222 (TTY: 1-866-290-4236). You must **call** from the phone number that you want to **register**. To **register** online (**donotcall**.gov), you **will** have to respond to a confirmation email.

Sadly, it hasn't helped at all. Salespeople are annoying because our brains are wired to flee from persuasive scenarios. Those that force us to do things that are unnatural are difficult to trust.

## Visnostics is how to sell without getting the negative reaction that naturally occurs towards sales efforts.

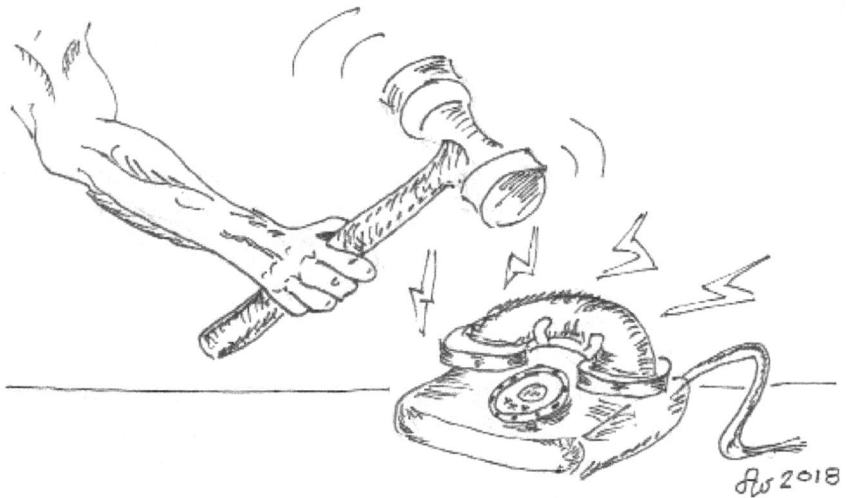

Do Not Call

With the "Fight or Flight" instinct in mind, it is important that these exercises are not conducted without an explanation that will ensure that your participant's defensive walls are down. Please inform your participant that you are doing an experiment from a book you are reading. Then ask if they would please help you by participating by responding to a few statements.

Remember that most people enjoy an opportunity to help as long as there isn't a catch or a hidden agenda.

## Fight your Flight instincts and do these exercises!

_____

# The Power of Visualization

What does Visualization mean to you? Visualization is often described using several words like conversion, translation, interpretation, and envisioning. What if your vision is different than what your client is envisioning? Translating is hard work as well as risky because it can lead to misinterpretation. It is the biggest reason for lost sales and even lost clients.

Word such as "considerable," "extensive," "immediate," or "quickly" are subjective and can cause miscommunication between you and your client. You could be setting yourself up for a future dissatisfied client. In addition, slang, acronyms and industry jargon are dangerous. **Visnostics will help you translate!**

# A Different Type of Christmas Story

I want to share a story of a deal I lost due to two different visions of what my company could do for a client.

There was a time when companies needed to migrate data from one device to another device. To do this, companies had to bring down production to do a migration and holidays were a common time to do this due to low activity. I sold software that allowed companies to do this migration while production was live. Needless to say, this was a pretty easy sale.

I was in Dallas at a major retailer's headquarters and I had already done a lot of homework. One of the men was a technical influencer and he mentioned to me that he hadn't been home with his family on Christmas Day in years. He explained that he would watch his children open their gifts and then head to the office for the rest of the day. I couldn't wait to give him the good news! He would never miss Christmas with his family ever again!

I thought I nailed the presentation! So you can imagine my shock at how quickly I was told that I would not be winning their business. I went back to their office to find out what I did wrong. To my surprise, the man that told me about working Christmas Day admitted that he killed the deal.

His reason was very simple. He relied very heavily on the triple pay he got on Christmas Day to buy the gifts for his family each year. Therefore, he viewed our services as a threat, not a benefit. When he told me that he hadn't been home in years, I interpreted that as a bad thing. I found out too late that he actually depended on it and there were other days he got extra pay that my company and I would eliminate. In other words, my offering hurt him and his family personally! This was a very painful lesson about the risk involved when translating sales benefits to client benefits. I would have bet my commission check that he viewed me as his HEROINE, not his VILLAIN!

A great Visnostic Statement for this would have been, "I will never have to work on weekends or holidays ever again!" His reply would have been "Not important, not applicable, or I don't know" which would have been a huge indicator for me to get clarification from the client BEFORE I went in with guns-a-blazing about how he would get to spend Christmas with his family!

---

There are at least two types of translation that take place during a sales cycle. Salespeople are trying to map their products and services to the pain and need of the client and the client is trying to interpret how the features and functions of the vendor's offering will convert to his or her world. This is a universal issue and yet we continue to handle it poorly.

## We need to take the translation risks out of the sales cycle.

Visualization Diagnostic Statements will flush out these important facts before you ever even present to your client!

---

# EXERCISE #1
# The Power of Visualization

This is very simple to do and it works every single time!

In 2007, I was part of a transformation team that toured the country teaching "Order Takers" how to be "Hunters." I began my presentation with a little exercise that I want you to try before you read any further.

I don't know where you are right now. You may be on a plane, or reading this in bed before you go to sleep, or on a lunch break. It doesn't matter where you are right now; what matters is that you have an innocent bystander that you can nab and ask him or her to participate in an exercise that will take less than 15 seconds.

If you are alone, DO NOT be tempted to pick up the phone to call someone because it is important that you watch the participant's eyes. After you explain this is an experiment, just say these simple words –

*"I am going to say a word and I need you to tell me the first VISUAL that pops into your head. What is the first thing you SEE when you hear this word…."*

## (Pause)  Are you ready? (Pause)
## "MONEY"

## Be sure to carefully watch the eyes.

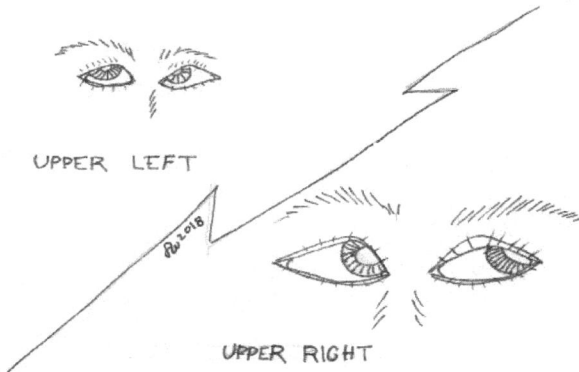

UPPER LEFT

UPPER RIGHT

The eyes will move rather fast so if you blink, you may miss it. Often, you will see them look up to the right or up to the left. As sales professionals, we should know the basics of body language and this means they are thinking and visualizing something.

Ask them to be as detailed as possible when describing what they see. It's incredible how fast our minds visualize memories. Please send me an email describing what they say to you to this email address – money@dynaexec.com.

It is important that you follow these instructions because emailing me a description of what happened will help reinforce what you saw and learned. Those that skip this step will not improve as much as those that take time to reflect, envision, and document the observations of this exercise.

## Lessons Learned From Exercise #1

There are so many lessons to be learned by doing this exercise.

One lesson is that our minds visualize things extremely fast when it is something to which we can relate.

Another lesson is that different minds process data differently. For example, I often get short answers during this exercise but every once in a while; a person will describe what sounds like a movie! Sometimes when I ask what a person visualizes, instead, they describe FEELINGS.

I was with a lady that I have hired three different times. She is the best salesperson and relationship builder I have ever met. However, I consistently had challenges keeping her focused. I always assumed it was because she has been diagnosed with ADD.

As we reviewed the draft of this book together, I became very aware that her brain moves faster and with many more details than other people. What she described to me when she heard the word "Money" was extremely emotional and thorough. She described money as being a source of freedom and then gave me multiple examples. The word triggered more emotions from her than any other person I have ever encountered. Her explanation went on for over ten minutes and her eyes were darting in every direction.

I realized that not only did I get an understanding of how she views the word "money,' I also got an education on how different her thought process is compared to other people that have done this exercise with me. I was seeing firsthand how difficult it is for a person with such an active brain to be focused on one thing at a time.

I realized that I needed to be aware of how her brain processes information and visualizes conversations so I can understand how I might want to adjust my own communication style with her. This will be enlightening as you get to know new clients as well. As she was talking, I wondered how many brains like hers have been diagnosed as having ADD when in reality their brains are much more active than other brains. To me, what I was witnessing was a gift or talent versus a handicap or disability as ADD is often viewed.

A few weeks later, I did this same exercise with a relative and she said she has so many negative feelings around the word money. She also went into great detail about the bad feelings that surfaced when she heard this word.

## Words can trigger unexpected emotional responses.

Both of these ladies described **feelings** when they heard the word versus an **image**. One responded positively emotionally and the other responded negatively. The word was the same but the responses and perceptions were complete opposites. Why does this matter? Those of you that watched the video I recommended in the Introduction will know exactly why this is important to understand.

If you are presenting, you are assuming that your audience comprehends your message the way you intend it to be received. But how can you determine if you are accomplishing this goal? How do you determine how your client is processing information? Those that visualize a movie may have a more challenging time keeping up during a fast-paced presentation. This reaction may cause you to lose important points with some members of your audience.

What if I told you that Visnostic Statements will ensure that your clients communicate their interpretation of your messaging? This will enable you to avoid miscommunication from occurring.

**Getting your audience to visualize and articulate their current situation is the most impactful way to get them emotionally engaged in your conversation. Their comments will also validate their comprehension of the points you are making.**

During this exercise, the more details your participant gives you, the more emotional engagement you will observe. The eyes will reveal additional emotions and you can observe the magnitude of the visualizations taking place in their mind.
Now let's discuss why most people will resist following the instructions around this exercise.

While writing and sharing with a test group, not one person followed the instructions or shared their experience with me via email as requested. This in itself is proof that when someone feels they are being coerced or persuaded to do something, the natural instinct is to rebel and flee. It was simply too much work for the reader. So why do we expect a different response from our clients? Translating is hard work. That makes it very risky for sales because it can lead to misinterpretations by your clients.

**The more work you do for the client, the more you will be perceived as adding value and the more receptive your client will be to your message.**

I did this exercise with one of my favorite recruiters and she told me that she saw an orange. Because that was the first time I had ever heard that response, I asked her to elaborate on why she saw an orange. She explained that money buys her food and she loves oranges. So this conversation with my recruiter is even more evidence of how one single word can mean so many different things to many different people. As salespeople, one of our biggest challenges is to understand how our audience is interpreting our words.

**Words translate differently because we each have different experiences. One single word can mean different things triggering completely different emotions within each person.**

I recall many conversations I have had with clients over the years where we had communication challenges. Often, their interpretations of industry terms such as "the cloud" or "implementation" were very different than my company or mine.

When I wrote my first book, I decided I wanted to leverage a Publisher. I learned quickly that my vision of the role a Publisher would play in my life was very different than the vision my Publisher had. This different expectation of what a Publisher is has caused a great deal of disappointment for both of us.

I'm sure you can think of a communication breakdown you've had recently due to different interpretations of what words meant. In fact, any married person should have LOTS of stories!

As I described in an earlier story, even working on Christmas Day can have different perspectives and produce different emotional responses. Understanding your client's unique visualizations will help you exceed versus falling short of their expectations. You have probably heard that studies show most sales are lost due to a communication failure. Personally, I think this simplifies why most sales are lost but this communication breakdown is why this book is so important.

Wouldn't it be cool if you could get into your clients' heads? Once you are aware of their visualizations, you won't make the mistake of focusing on YOUR visions by accident as I did in my previous Christmas Day Story.

## Visnostic Statements flush out your clients' visualizations thus reducing the risk of communication misinterpretations, disappointments, disconnects, or breakdowns.

Too many times, the client's expectations do not match the salesperson's interpretations of those expectations.

These communication challenges often result in unnecessary lost sales. But this can be avoided with some simple changes to how we communicate.

I have conducted this exercise hundreds of times since 2007. Most people say they see physical items such as bags of money, coins, stacks of currency, and bags of gold. Others see symbols like a $ dollar, € Euro, ¥ Yen, or £ Pound. Some of the more creative and humorous responses I have heard are things like the alimony check I write each month, my mortgage payment, bills, my tuition payment, my home, my children, my spouse, my parents...the list goes on and on.

The main lesson learned in Exercise #1 may shock many readers but **there are no right or wrong answers when asked to describe what is visualized when hearing the word** *MONEY*. **This exercise demonstrated that each person will TRANSLATE or convert those letters into something meaningful that is unique to him or her.**

**Therefore, this exercise proves that presenting WHAT your company does and WHY it does it, is NOT effective and is high risk.   Your client's may not translate your words as you intended!**

## The biggest surprise in this exercise is not what people say in response. It is what they DON'T say that should make every single reader change the way in which he or she communicates.

Here is the part of Exercise #1 that should make those light bulbs start going off for many readers:

Despite receiving hundreds of different responses, not one single person has EVER said they saw a slide with a bullet and the LETTERS

# M

# O

# N

# E

# Y

We simply do not visualize letters or words. In fact, our brains are a lot like a computer. Computers convert 1's and 0's to something on the screen that we can comprehend.

---

## EXERCISE #2
## The Power of Translation

Below is a sentence written with binary code. You can search for "binary code translator" and type these numbers into it and it will automatically translate it for you. Email me at autosales@dynaexec.com and tell me what it says.

Less than 1% of you will be curious enough to figure out how to translate it. That means 99% of you will engage your flight instinct to justify avoiding that effort.

01010000 01100101 01101111 01110000 01101100
01100101 00100000 01100001 01110110 01101111
01101001 01100100 00100000 01110100 01110010
01100001 01101110 01110011 01101100 01100001
01110100 01101001 01101111 01101110 00100001

Our brains do the same thing when they convert letters to physical things that we can comprehend. Just as computers translate zeros and ones into letters and symbols, salespeople need to translate letters and words into visualization for our clients!

So my questions to each reader are:

## WHY DO WE KEEP PRESENTING SLIDES LOADED WITH BULLETS AND LETTERS?

———————

## WHY DO WEBSITES HAVE MORE WORDS THAN GRAPHICS?

———————

## WHY DO THE GRAPHICS NOT EVEN MATCH THE MESSAGE?

———————

## WHY ARE MOST BUSINESS BOOKS FULL OF WORDS YET VERY FEW PICTURES?

———————

## WHY CREATE ANY MARKETING MATERIALS LOADED WITH PICTURES THAT HAVE ZERO TO DO WITH THE TOPIC?

Your communication, presentations, websites, emails, and advertisements MUST have visuals and these visuals must tie back to your message...

...But only if you want your audience to Relate (understand), Retain (remember), and Repeat (give you referrals)

Does your message tell a story that helps ensure your client can Relate, Retain, and Repeat?

# These are the Three R's of Visualization Diagnostic Statements Relate - Retain – Repeat

With the "Three R's" in mind, let's stop for a moment and reflect on the first story in this book. Remember the roast story with the mother and daughter? As you read this, what did you visualize? Do you see the drawings or do you see the letters in the story?

What about the Christmas Story? Do you "see" the wreath? Do you remember the story?

What about the graphic with the little guy that had on boxing gloves and then another graphic of him running? What did that graphic represent?

You REMEMBER those stories, don't you? Neuroscience is so predictable and so universally effective. Why aren't we leveraging it in our communications with EVERYBODY?

I ask you again, "Why do our marketing materials, slides, brochures, websites, and infographics have so many words?" Why do we prefer to watch videos on YouTube instead of reading how to do something?

**The answer is that we want that visual translation done for us. We don't want our brains to do that**

**work. We are only human. And guess what? The last time I checked, our clients are human too.**

Ideally, marketing will create Visnostic messaging. However, if they don't, it is up to the salesperson to convert and translate those features and functions into something that the client can relate to, comprehend, understand, and VISUALIZE.

And guess what? When a salesperson is forced to do this, they aren't selling. Relying on sales to do this is a costly decision but it's the only way I've been able to convert features and functions into meaningful Visnostic content that my clients are craving.

This hasn't been marketing's fault; Visnostics aren't taught in college (YET) and most marketing teams won't learn Visnostics in a traditional marketing role. For marketing departments to stop the madness that is product marketing, they will have to change the way they operate.

When was the last time your marketing team interacted with your existing client base? How does marketing create case studies or track ROI (Return on Investments) with clients? As marketing departments become more interactive with clients, they may uncover unique ways clients benefit that are excluded in the current messaging. This has happened to me multiple times in my career!

The most common mistake I see sales and companies make is to list out all their features and functions with the expectation that the clients will accurately TRANSLATE those details into how it applies to their own world. Depending upon clients to make that translation is a huge mistake. It is extremely risky to assume your clients WANT to convert your presentation or if they even know how!

And some of the guiltiest professions around are related to the automobile industry! Do you ever have clients tell you exactly what they want and how much they want to spend? Of course they do, thanks to the internet! Do you sell them what they said they wanted? If you answered yes to this, why do you trust that they know what they want?

I suspect most of you reading this will want to respond with "I don't want to be pushy or annoy them." **VISNOSTICS KEP THIS FROM HAPPENING!**

## Your customers only know what they know; they don't know what they DON'T know!!

You may need to read that statement several times and let it sink in for a few minutes. As a Buyer, I am guilty of this almost every single time I've bought a car since the internet was invented. I like to do my homework before I walk into a dealership so I am confident that I know what I want. And guess what? Almost every single time, I later realize that there were brand new "toys" and "gadgets" that I was unaware of and if my salesperson had educated me...guess what I would have done? **I WOULD HAVE BOUGHT A MORE EXPENSIVE CAR!** I believe that most car salespeople today are missing a HUGE opportunity to UPSELL clients that come in saying that they know exactly what they want because salespeople BELIEVE THEM!

## If you try to give your customers what they THINK they want without using Visnostics first, you may be doing BOTH of you a huge injustice!

I can completely understand how the internet has made selling cars much easier today. However, if you find yourself selling a car based upon price or selling a car without taking time to educate your customer, that is one of the laziest forms of selling that there is. In fact, that isn't selling, that is ORDER TAKING.

The good news is that this is one of the easiest professions to fix, which is why this special edition was written. Chapter 2 is customized 100% for sales in the Automotive Industry.

Also as you read the next chapter, try and reflect on how many people you have talked with that told you what they thought they wanted yet bought something completely different. Can you articulate WHY that shift in their decision making occurred? It's not the Buyers fault when this happens; **it's actually the SALESPERSON'S responsibility to help them VISUALIZE what they truly want in their next car. They do this by fully EDUCATING them about everything available to ensure their next purchase will make them FEEL the very best when driving that vehicle.**

What clients WANT is often very different than what they THINK they want. If you talk with top salespeople, I'm confident they will agree that they try upfront to really understand their Buyers' VISIONS.

**The best Salespeople MATCH DREAMS to the right vehicles instead of selling cars the buyers THINK they want for the price they THINK they want to pay.**

---

## EXERCISE #3
## The Power of Translation (continued)

Post this on social media – *"What are the top five things you love about your current vehicle and why?"*

Collect the responses for a week and then copy and paste them in an email to autosales@dynaexec.com. I will respond with something very enlightening to demonstrate the difference between VENDOR-SPEAK and CLIENT-SPEAK.

## WE MUST SPEAK THE SAME LANGUAGE AND THAT LANGUAGE MUST BE CLIENT-SPEAK!

I can't wait to read the emails and messages about how these simple changes will positively impact your business!

I know you will enjoy the rest of the book!

# CHAPTER TWO –
## Special Edition - Visnostics for Car Sales

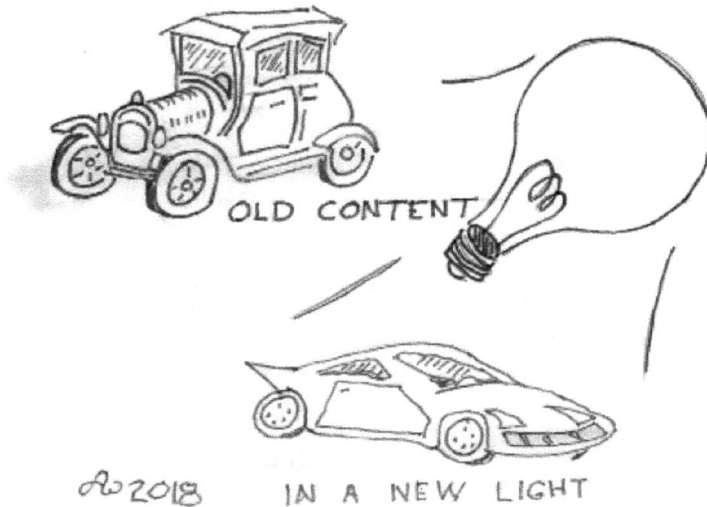

OLD CONTENT

𝒜ℴ 2018    IN A NEW LIGHT

Assuming that you are in the Auto Industry, and assuming that you are reading this book because you are in sales or hope to be in sales someday, I want to describe a scenario for you:

You are sitting in your office at the dealership, looking out the window, when you see a woman walk up to one of the cars on your lot. She is looking at the window sticker and walking around the vehicle. You get up from your desk and walk in her direction.

## What are the first words you say as you approach her?

Do you ask how she is doing?
Do you introduce yourself?
Do you ask how you can help her?
These are the three main ways salespeople have approached me in the past and each time I wanted to tell the salesperson to leave me alone. But I'm polite so what do you think my response was?

How about, "I'm just looking." Which is a polite way of saying, "Go away."

Has this happened to you? Have you ever wondered why people are not more receptive to your attempts to talk to them?

Well first of all, nobody believes a salesperson really wants to know how they are doing. So asking that question is actually quite insulting and counterproductive. And introducing yourself comes off as incredibly arrogant because YOU walked up to the customer, not the other way around. Why would you think the customers care who you are? And then asking how you can help them is another annoyance because customers know that what you really mean is "Can I sell you a car and make myself some commissions?" All three of these approaches will trigger the "Fight or Flight" instinct. Some people are just better at masking their true thoughts and feelings. But it IS there.

All these realities are why people become defensive or dismissive to you when you approach them. And they are actually EXPECTING those words to come out of your mouth because salespeople can be so predictable! Like the Roast Story read in the introduction – why are you doing what everybody else has done for the past one hundred years? Why not be different?

## Instead, what if you walked up and asked her to tell you her story?

That sounds weird and it is. But there is science behind why it will work. People LOVE to hear their own voice. People LOVE to share their own stories. And by asking them for their story, you are actually taking an interest in them personally. AND it is not at all what they are expecting from a salesperson; so they will drop their guard.

In fact, as you are approaching them, they are subconsciously preparing their response to one of those three questions they are always asked. So when you do something different, they really don't have time to plan an avoidance response so chances are high they will actually answer your question and tell you their story.

Furthermore, you will be fascinated by the number of different responses you will get. Remember the "MONEY" exercise? I highly recommend you do that exercise as many times as you can just so you can see for yourself how diverse the responses and emotions can be.

If you didn't do it, you missed out on a VERY important understanding of Visnostics; every person is unique and every person will react differently based upon their experiences. And salespeople need to work hard to destroy the selfish perceptions that many people have of them.

Dale Carnegie published a book in the 1920's called, *How to Win Friends and Influence People*. It is the best book I have ever read. It basically teaches that nobody likes you because of how awesome you are. They like you because of how they feel when they are around you. And how do you get them to feel good when they are around you? **GET THEM TO TALK ABOUT THEMSELVES!**

The problem with salespeople is that they are trained to talk about their company, their products, the features, the functions, and the price of what they sell. So they are programmed to talk about the wrong things!

## THIS IS NOT WHY PEOPLE BUY! SO WHY DO WE CONTINUE TO DO THIS?

Recently, a salesperson in the automotive industry told me that Visnostics don't apply to his business because customers buy cars based upon the research they do prior to arriving to the dealership.

This has been such a fun part of having a best-selling book. I see that Fight of Flight instinct kicked in every single day and in new ways. So many salespeople create their own failures due to self-inflicted mental barriers. Why do we tend to talk ourselves into believing something won't work? The full terminology is actually Fight, Flight, or FREEZE. And avoidance is a form of the FREEZE instinct and only YOU can control that destructive behavior.

So if anybody reading this is skeptical or still doesn't see how to execute, I implore you to stop reading and reach out to me NOW and let's discuss! I sincerely enjoy hearing as many perspectives as possible because I learn something new every day listening to other sales professionals describe how they are applying Visnostics to their particular industry. I CAN help you be successful with the new communication approach.

———————

Remember Exercise #3? You didn't do it, did you? Well, I did it for you just in case that silly avoidance instinct was uncontrollable.

I asked my own contacts, *"What are the top five things you love about your current vehicle and why?"*

Here is just a sample of some of the responses –

**CLIENT SPEAK –**
I live in New York and I love my Subaru Forester because it is good to drive in the snow, it is reliable, it has plenty of heat in the winter, the back seats go down flat, it is all–wheel–drive.

I live in New York and I love my Ford F250, diesel 4x4, crew cab truck because it is reliable, has plenty of heat in the winter, carries massive amounts of stuff, hauls my hay and horse trailer, and it is high enough to see ahead more clearly.

I love my 2011 Acura TSX because it is sporty, sunroof, leather, heated seats and air conditioning.

I love my 2012 Dodge 2500 Diesel truck because I had it built like I wanted. Leather seats are heated. I raised it about 3ft. It has big tires and Ranch Hand bumpers front and back. It has air suspension in rear to help with towing our RV.

I love my Honda Goldwing Trike because it helps me feel the breeze hot or cold and clears my mind.

**VENDOR SPEAK –**
Engine size/Horsepower, Vehicle Dimensions, Miles Per Gallon, Color, Weight, Wheels, just to name a few.

Are you starting to see the difference? SPECS are NOT why people buy the car. Did you notice how the owners tend to describe how they USE the vehicle? For example, it may be All-Wheel-Drive but the reason they love that feature is because it can tackle rough terrain and inclement weather scenarios. Instead of throwing out a spec and expecting the client to translate it into how they will use it, we must do WHAT??????

## TRANSLATE
## FOR
## THEM!

Remember the Binary Code in Exercise #2? To date, less than 10 readers (out of THOUSANDS of books sold) have emailed me the translation of that binary code. In fact, I'd estimate that 80% of the people that bought one of my books, haven't even read it yet!

## My point is that almost everybody wants to be successful but few are willing to put in the effort.

So how can you get your customers to ponder an upsell without triggering the fight or flight or the laziness that resides in each of us? The answer is to educate them without blasting them with a bunch of questions. You must find a way to educate your audience without making them FEEL like you are attempting an upsell!

By the time you finish Chapter Three, you will have a very clear understanding of how you can communicate with customers without ever sounding like a salesperson.

Most of my books are written from the salesperson's perspective but since I have never sold any type of auto but I HAVE purchased several types of items with engines, this chapter will be written 100% from a Buyer's perspective. I expect future editions will have more input from Salespeople's' successes as I gather stories from future readers.

In fact, I'm counting on it because readers have given me some of the most valuable content for my books! As you continue reading, when you feel" inspired," please email your thoughts to autosales@dynaexec.com.

# CHAPTER THREE –
## Why People REALLY Buy Autos

Eight years ago, I was driving a BMW 5-series and when it was time for service, as most people do, I took it back to the dealership.

My check-engine light kept coming on and they couldn't figure out what was wrong with it. I took it back three different times. The third time, they kept it for an entire month and gave me a Mini-Cooper as a loaner. Seriously? Why would they give a luxury vehicle owner a loaner that was nothing like their own vehicle? It felt like I was driving a golf cart for a month.

Sorry if this offends any Mini-Cooper owners reading this but I was not a fan of the driving experience and I was certainly not a fan of this dealerships service department.

I knew I needed to make a change. First, I looked at different BMW service departments but they were so far away! The next option was to start researching other automobiles. But I found myself more interested in the quality of service departments than about what types of cars were sold.

During this research, I became intrigued with a dealership that had won the Malcolm Baldrige National Quality Award, which is the highest level of national recognition for excellence. THIS sounded like an experience that would be completely opposite of the one I was currently dealing with. AND the dealership was in a better, safer location and substantially closer to my home than the BMW dealership. Needless to say, I was eager to find a car I liked from this new company.

I found a car online that interested me because it was a hybrid. Based upon the research I did on the Internet, I decided that I really wanted a part electric and part gas car. I hadn't made any solid decisions but this was definitely on my radar in a big way.

So when I got the call that my car was finally ready, I dropped everything to go pick it up. However, I wasn't even out of the parking lot before every light on my dashboard lit up! It scared me, but I was furious at the same time. I went back inside and smoke had to have been coming out of my nose and ears because my service manager looked at me with horror. If looks could kill, he would have exploded into a million pieces as I made eye contact with him.

I had to sit in their lobby another 30 minutes waiting to find out what was wrong this time. Guess what was wrong? My service manager informed me that they neglected to put any of the fluids back into my car! Are you kidding me?! I had to sit there for an additional hour while they filled up the oils and other fluids that I know nothing about and then test it.

When I got my car for the second time that day, the engine light came on! That was the original reason I brought the car in a month ago and two other times before that. This place was incompetent.

That Malcolm Baldrige winner was looking REAL good at this moment. The BMW service department offered to keep my car and let me keep driving the Mini-Cooper. I told them that I was done with them and with BMW. Can you believe that they still charged me over $500 after all that? I'm shocked that I let them off so easily.

At this point, I just wanted to ditch this nightmare of a car. I literally (this term is used incorrectly all the time but I'm actually using it correctly) drove directly to the Malcolm Baldrige winner and walked up to the first salesperson I made eye contact with and told her that this was going to be the easiest sale of her life!

During that additional hour I was at the dealership waiting for them to put fluids in my car, I made a list of everything I loved about my BMW. I handed her my list and she did something on her computer and she said she had two cars in stock with those options. They were both the same color so I did my obligatory test drive around the block and told her this is what I wanted and I wanted to trade my BMW in (which was completely paid off). I was out of there in thirty minutes with my new car and most of that time was the sales lady going over all the new gadgets on the car that I didn't even have on my BMW. I was thrilled with my very spontaneous and emotional decision-making process.

If you've ever heard that people buy based upon emotions, well I just gave you the poster-child example of an emotional purchase!

I had that car for four years. I have to admit that I missed the "quality" feel of the BMW. Like when I shut the door of the BMW, it just felt really solid and expensive. The backs of the seats were leather on the BMW but this new car had a lot of plastic on the backs of the seats. Overall, this new car felt more lightweight and less expensive. So I didn't get that same feeling of "success" when I drove it. The gas mileage of the hybrid was much better than the BMW so I really liked that cost savings a lot. And that meant I wasn't filling up my care every three days. Instead, I was filling up about once every two weeks. So for everything I disliked about my new car, there were many other things that made up for them.

In summary, I wouldn't say that I loved the car but I definitely loved the service department and I was thrilled that the pain and stress I was dealing with at the BMW dealership was completely gone.

Despite being a BMW Dealership, the waiting room was comprised of some very uncomfortable plastic chairs setup in the middle of the showroom. The only perk was one of those coffee machines that brewed pods. It was pretty obvious that they hoped the customers that were waiting for their service to be completed would get up from those uncomfortable chairs and go look at the newer models and maybe even buy one.

In contrast, this new place was like going to a country club or the Admirals Club at the airport. It had private cubicles with phones and Internet for those that wanted to do work while there. HGTV was playing on a 70-inch TV with an incredible selection of plush furniture. One day while I was there, I saw an employee going around fluffing the pillows that were on each chair! The coffee machine was a computer that was like a robotic barista that would make any type of fancy coffee drink you wanted. I actually looked forward to bringing my car in to get an oil change and was disappointed when my car was ready! It truly is the best service center I've ever been to in my entire life. They even provided free carwashes even if you didn't need service. They had an app that had huge discounts of luxury items and services. They even provided a window sticker that got owners free valet parking at sporting events! It was very obvious why they earned the Malcolm Baldrige award for quality service. They were a breath of fresh air to me! In fact, I wondered how the BMW dealership stayed in business with this as their competitor!

Despite not feeling that my car was as luxurious, I actually bought the latest model of the exact same car again! And I would have purchased it from my original sales lady but it was four years later and she no longer worked there.

You are probably wondering how Visnostics has anything to do with this story. Well, as pleasant and efficient as that sales lady made my purchase that day; she could have and should have sold me a completely different vehicle!

## It took me four years to realize her mistake; which in reality was BOTH our mistake!

When I bought the second model four years later, there was a brand-new feature that wasn't on my first vehicle that is a game changer (in my opinion). And it is such an incredible feature that I cannot live without it now that I know it exists! It is such a wonderful enhancement that I will no longer even drive RENT CARS that don't have this feature! And while it didn't exist on the model I purchased four years earlier, a more expensive vehicle DID have that feature and I would have gladly paid the additional $20,000 four years ago had I known about it!

What is this magical new feature?

Well we all know what cruise control is and I'm sure just about every reader has used cruise control during his or her driving career.

What are the most annoying behaviors that come to mind when you are on a long road trip and you are trying to enjoy that cruise control function? How about when you are cruising along with the appropriate car lengths between you and the car in front of you and then suddenly someone decides to pull in front of you to fill up one of your car lengths forcing you to slam on the brakes and disengage the cruise control?

Or what about those drivers that can't manage to maintain a consistent speed and gradually slow down just as the lanes around you are full of cars so you can't simply pass around them? Again, forcing you to disengage the cruise control.

Well, with "Radar" (also known as Adaptive Cruise Control – ACC) the two sudden braking scenarios I just described are no longer an issue. I quickly learned that ACC systems use on-board sensors and software that automatically manage the distance between your vehicle and the vehicle that you're following. The ACC system maintains a preset following distance by controlling vehicle speed and applying the brakes when necessary. How cool is THAT?!

And after getting spoiled with ACC on my current vehicle for two years, I will never own another vehicle without this wonderful feature! It's almost as though the car is driving without me or at least it feels like I have a copilot that is focused on our safety.

There are other things this new model does that the older one didn't do that are all safety related. For example, I can turn on a feature that alerts me if I sway too close to the other lane.

Even if I don't have my radar feature on, if the car in front of me suddenly brakes, my car responds by breaking too. Both of these options were available when I purchase the original model of my car but I would have had to buy a more expensive car. I WOULD HAVE DONE THAT!

## I only knew what I knew and I didn't know what I didn't know!

And if I didn't know about it, how could I ask for it? That list I gave my sales lady was a list of things I knew I wanted. What about all the things I didn't KNOW I WANTED?? **The ability to educate your buyers is what will separate the Super Stars from the average car salespeople.** And you obviously want to be a superstar or you wouldn't have bought this book. So let's do this!

I emailed, called, and messaged people on LinkedIn from dozens of different dealerships and explained that I am writing a book and I needed the following information:

1. **What is the number one car people come in and say they want to buy?**
2. **What car is the car that all the salespeople dream of selling?**
3. **What features does that dream car have that no other cars have?**
4. **What are some quotes from happy customers that bought the dream car?**

I wanted to ensure that this part of the book was fair, so I made a conscious effort to contact luxury dealerships but I also contacted dealerships that are average prices and even economy dealerships.

Apparently, the Fight or Flight instinct kicked in with every salesperson except one. Because only one person responded and I am going to give him a mini commercial to thank him for his effort. While the next few pages may seem as though this book is intended to sell Cadillacs, it is NOT. This was the only response I received. If you'd like me to do the same thing for you and what you sell, reach out to me and I'm happy to walk through this process with you.

Tim, if you are reading this, be sure and email me when you start selling even more cars because of the case study I'm about to build around your responses. And to those of you that allowed your Fight or Flight to kick in when I asked you for your input, I hope you are kicking another part of your body right now...

# Tim P. Tillapaugh
# 239.825.7711 Cell

## What is the number one car people come in and say they WANT to buy?

*Our Best-Selling Vehicle is the Cadillac XT5. Although, for those that want the "Ultimate Luxury" the Cadillac Escalade is the way to go. for 20 years, the Cadillac Escalade has led automotive design, with opulence and function fit for only the grandest stage. from a striking design aesthetic, to a comfortable and accommodating cabin that is as spacious as it is versatile. The 2020 Cadillac Escalade offers nothing but the best.*

Side Note: Can you tell his response was written by marketing? Look at all those fluffy words – opulence, grandest stage, striking design aesthetic...STOP THIS MADNESS! NOBODY, AND I MEAN NOBODY is going to walk up and use those words to describe why they bought a car. In addition, many of these words are subjective. Remember the MONEY exercise? These words mean different things to different people. VENDOR SPEAK is so ineffective! Send this book to that marketing team! They NEED help!

### What car is the car that all the salespeople dream of selling?
*The 2020 Cadillac Escalade*

### What Features does that dream car have that no other cars have?
*Safety features like Collison Alert, Lane Assist, Self-Braking, Night Vison, Super Cruise. Also comfort features like Heated & Ventilated Seats, Heated Steering Wheel, Massage Seats & a Sunroof*

Another Side Note: Are you seeing the problem without me pointing it out? Marketing strikes again. "Collision Alert" "Lane Assist" "Super Cruise" – all marketing buzz words. Clients will have to search those words to understand what exactly they will get and why they should even care.

### What are some quotes from happy customers that bought the dream car?
*Tim P. Tillapaugh was very professional and he wasn't the "pushy" sales type. He was a Consultant. It was the Best Car Buying Experience we ever had. I will definitely recommend Tim to my family & friends, who are looking to buy a Vehicle.*

Thank you, Tim, for such a great response. To those of you reading that are experienced auto sales people, his responses to those questions probably sounds about right. Tim is responding exactly how he has been trained to respond. He is using the tools that the company gave him. Those tools are the words created by a very educated and well-paid marketing team so why wouldn't he trust that they are the right words?

But from a CUSTOMER perspective the responses are full of marketing buzz words and fluff that just wastes customers time; I now have to do a lot of mental work to determine why I should care. And this book has proven over and over again that none of us want to have to do that extra work. So, these responses COULD setup a scenario for a lost sale.

One final comment about his responses regarding his answer to the 4th question. The quotes from happy clients I was looking for were about their vehicle purchased, not the salesperson. This is another very common thing ALL salespeople (and marketing people) do naturally; which is to focus on himself or herself versus the client. While there is a ton of sales training available that focuses on relationship selling, people forget something very important;

## They may buy from you because they like you, but if they buy the same car again, it's because they liked the CAR!

Remember the story I told you about my current car? I went back to the same dealership to buy the same car. The sales lady I bought from four years earlier had left the company. I didn't bother tracking her down. I wanted the CAR, not the salesperson.

Furthermore, if I consider the experience I had with my BMW, if that salesperson ever ended up at the dealership I liked, and sold the car I wanted, I would actually go out of my way to get another salesperson. Why? It wasn't HIS fault that the service department was terrible. But the entire experience triggers the same response as Pavlov's Dog. We all know this story; Pavlov fed a dog a steak but before he did it, he rang a bell. After that conditioning, every time the dog heard a bell, he salivated because he related the bell to getting a steak. Therefore, it supports this comment:

**Customers may buy from you because they like you but if they end up regretting their purchase, you will become guilty by association and the relationship will often self-destruct.**

So how does a salesperson ensure that they trigger a positive memory and ensure every client relates them to a great experience? The magic happens when a salesperson takes the features and functions mentioned in this response and does the translating for the customer! For example, why do customers care about Collision Alert? What is super about "Super Cruise?" So many vehicles have heated and cooled seats today so what are these different or better than the other models? This may be difficult to understand at this point of the book, but once a salesperson does that translation from Vendor–Speak to Client–Speak, it releases a reaction in the brain that is similar to serotonin. And just as Pavlov's dog related the bell to something good was about to happen, your clients will have that same reaction to their salesperson!

So let's get back to how to do this translation...

**When was the last time you called a past customer to ask him or her what are the top five things they love about the automobile they purchased from you?**

# When was the last time your salesperson called YOU to ask YOU those same questions?

What do your past customers say about the reasons they love their new vehicles? For example, I purchased my second hybrid because I feel safer driving a car that I am familiar with. But after a few months of owning it, I loved it for all the new features that I didn't think I wanted. This is a VERY important point! But that is typically where salespeople stop. Don't accept this answer! Dig Deeper!

With Visnostics, you will change the way you THINK. You will change the way you COMMUNICATE. And you will naturally pickup on that I am not giving you the right answer when I say, "I just said I loved it for all the new features that I didn't think I wanted." I am way too vague in my responses. Dig it out of me with Visnostics! In this chapter you will learn something VERY powerful called RTH. I'm going to get you there slowly to ensure you truly understand this translation process and will be effective doing it TODAY!

There are two very important reasons that all salespeople should check on their clients a few months after the purchase:

1. **You send a sincere message that you really DO care about your customers because they know you have spent that commission check a long time ago and no longer have a personal agenda.**
2. **You will learn more about how to properly sell that vehicle from the people that drive it every day, than you will ever learn from your own company and marketing team!**

**And yet very few salespeople will do those two very important steps because most salespeople just PRETEND to like their customers when all they really like is that commission check!**

# DON'T BE THAT PERSON!

---

Now let's get started on the Translation Process. This is where you will take Vendor–Speak and convert it to Client–Speak:

The first things we have to determine are SEGMENTATIONS.

As you may recall from the first part of this book, Segmentations are basically a way to categorize the topics for your Visnostic Statements. Tim sent me a separate email explaining that they have something called S.P.A.C.E.D. It stands for Safety, Performance, Appearance, Comfort, Convenience, Economy, and Dependability, Durability. And while these are great segmentations, I'm going to simplify things for this example, by consolidating those segments into just three areas:

1. **Driver Experience**
2. **Safety**
3. **Sales Experience**

The second things I look for are RESULTS. I don't see any results in Tim's comments above so I went to go to the internet to try and find some customer testimonials. The sources I used were:

https://www.caranddriver.com/cadillac/xt5
https://www.edmunds.com/cadillac/xt5/
https://cars.usnews.com/cars-trucks/cadillac/xt5
https://www.motortrend.com/cars/cadillac/xt5/
https://www.rippyautomotive.com/CadillacOwnerBenefits
https://www.YouTube.com

NOTE: While customers are doing a lot more research today than they did before the World Wide Web became a way of life, it is highly doubtful they will be willing to go to the extreme I went to for this book. Which explains why I keep saying that they will LOVE you if you do this translation work for them!

Another VERY important point regarding customer research – Studies have shown that people researching often uncover reasons NOT to buy and from what I'm reading so far, these reviews are highly critical. For this exercise, I am ignoring negative comments because I am searching for positive RESULTS. I'm finding that even the people writing these articles need some lessons in Visnostics. These articles are full of features and functions and truly do force the readers (aka your potential new customers) to try and figure out why they should care.

In the Introduction section of this book, I mentioned how our attention spans are shrinking. You have between 3 and 7

seconds to capture your audience's attention. So you MUST make sure
those first three words are compelling and are written in CLIENT– SPEAK versus VENDOR–SPEAK. That means your first few words MUST answer the following questions –

# WHY DO THEY CARE?
# WHAT ARE THE RESULTS?
# HOW WILL THEIR LIFE BE BETTER?

Finding results that translated into "why customers care about these features" was virtually impossible. The auto Industry has a lot of room for improvement in areas outside of sales. Marketing needs to ditch the marketing fluff and jargon. And these people being paid to write reviews need to translate features and functions into something the readers will understand. I don't know the statistics but if readership at these internet sites are down, I can see why! I got no value from these reviews because the authors of these articles communicated just like the dealerships, and the dealerships communicated just like the manufacturers.

## None of these sources of information communicated like people that actually purchased the vehicles!

In fact, I've had to TRANSLATE every single one of these statements MYSELF to explain client USAGE versus Features and Functions. I have bolded the first three words because these are the closest things I could come up with that are RESULTS experienced by the Buyers.

Notice that the following sentences (they aren't Visnostic Statements yet!) are categorized by the three SEGMENTATIONS I identified earlier.

## 1. Driver Experience/Results of the Cadillac XT5–

- **SAVE MONEY** because it is one of the most affordable and luxurious vehicles in its class.
- **FEEL SUCCESSFUL** driving the Cadillac Brand
- **DRIVERS MOVE QUICKLY** with the twin–turbo V–6.
- **XT5 OWNERS WILL LOVE HIGHWAY ON-RAMPS** due to 6.6 second 0–to–60–mph time.
- **PASSING IS EFFORTLESS** with VSeries
- **SMOOTH AND AIRY RIDE** even over rough surfaces with adaptive suspension
- **NEVER GET INTO A HOT OR COLD CAR AGAIN** with the auto start button located on the key. No app needed like other luxury vehicles.
- **WINTER WEATHER IS A BREEZE** with all-wheel drive option. **NEVER TOUCH A GAS CAP AGAIN** with the easy gas access. **PARALELL PARK LIKE A PRO EVERYTIME** with all the parking sensors and auto parking function.
- **ELIMINATE ALL THE CHARGING CORDS** with a high–powered wireless charging pad.
- **EASY PARKING BRAKE** with just a button versus a lever.
- **NEVER HAVE COLD HANDS** due to automatic steering wheel heater.
- **NO MORE FIGHTING OVER RIDING SHOTGUN** due to back seats charging ports, seat warmers, reclining seats, arm rests, and cup holders.
- **PROTECT YOUR PHONE** by storing it in a secret compartment that will charge and phone is fully controlled by touch screen.

- **YOUR FRIENDS WILL LOVE WHEN YOU DRIVE** because no more standing around waiting for the doors to unlock due to the keyless door locks. Two pushes of the door button unlocks all doors.
- **BUY THOSE SKIS OR TALL FLOOR LAMPS** – deep trunk with optional door for pass through back seat for long objects.
- **NEVER SWEAT OR FREEZE** with heated and air–conditioned seats.
- **TRAVEL IN EXTREME COMFORT** due to smooth ride, quiet cabin, and luxurious feeling with high–quality materials throughout.
- **SMART PURCHASE DUE TO GREAT VALUE** with many standard luxury features.
- **CADILLAC OWNERS ARE HAPPY** with all the luxury–minded details.
- **MAXIMIZE YOUR LUGGAGE** due to large improved cargo capacity with folding rear seatbacks.
- **DRIVE TIME IS MORE COMFORTABLE AND PLEASANT** with front Massage seats.
- **TRAFFIC IS MORE BEARABLE** due to infotainment system.
- **ENOUGH ROOM** for seven carry–on bags due to extra–large cargo rear overhang that is larger than competitors

## 2. Safety of the Cadillac XT5 –
- **FEELS LIKE HAVING AN ADDITIONAL DRIVER** – with surround–view camera and other self-driving functions.
- **LIVE LONGER** because SURVIVOR XT5 did well on its crash testing

- **LIMIT FUTURE REPAIR AND MAINTENANCE EXPENSES** with one of the best 70,000-mile powertrain warranties.

### 3. Sales Experience of the Cadillac XT5 -
- *Tim P. Tillapaugh was very professional and he wasn't the "pushy" sales type. He was a Consultant. It was the Best Car Buying Experience we ever had. I will definitely recommend Tim to my family & friends, who are looking to buy a vehicle.*

While this is a great endorsement of Tim, if clients are truly happy with their vehicle purchase, they will be like me, and return to buy another vehicle. What if Tim leaves and is now selling a different type of vehicle at a different dealership? Does this mean that customers will track him down and buy whatever he is selling? I'm sure this happens but it is extremely rare.

What is more common, is that a return customer is coming back to buy the VEHICLE, not the salesperson. Why DO Cadillac owners keep buying more Cadillacs? Knowing this will make you a better sales professional. Yet this was difficult to find online.

The following points came from a dealership site that I can tell is trying hard to translate for their prospective clients. The site is rippyautomotive.com:

- **AMERICAN QUALITY** – The car is made by the most passionate people with the best equipment possible.
- **EXCLUSIVE OWNER BENEFITS** - Receive a comprehensive suite of owner benefits unmatched by any other automotive brand with Cadillac Shield.

- **A+ RATING WITH THE BETTER BUSINESS BUREAU**.

NOW, I am going to create a few tables organized again by SEGMENTATION. I am now going to create a few VISNOSTIC STATEMENTS from the translations I attempted.

# A Visnostic Statement is ALWAYS written as though your clients are saying them. This is critical. You will not have the same responses if you say" YOU will feel so successful driving a Cadillac!

Visnostic means VISualization DiagNOSTIC. So by stating things in the FIRST PERSON (Client–Speak) as though they are the ones making the statement, and then asking them for a response by selecting one of THREE responses (The Power of THREES**!), they will be focused on every single word you say, VISUALIZE their current situation, then VISUALIZE how their current situation can potentially IMPROVE,** and then be quiet. Let them talk as long as they want. Some people will surprise you how much they will share. This is due to the brain's reaction to this approach.

The first time you see this actually work, your life will change!!!

Please choose one of these three responses to each statement below.

- **I can say this today!**
- **I WISH I could say this today!**
  or
- **It's not important, not applicable, or I don't know.**

## DRIVER EXPERIENCE

| |
|---|
| I feel successful when driving my vehicle. |
| I never have to sit in a vehicle and wait for it to get warm or cool off. |
| I love getting a massage while I am driving. |
| I have no trouble getting to the necessary speed to enter a highway. |
| I never lose my cell phone while driving because it is securely charging in its own compartment. |
| My friends think I spent a lot more on my car than I did! |
| I no longer wear gloves while driving my car in the winter due to the steering wheel hand warmer. |
| I'm not wasting money on service thanks to my 70,000-mile warranty. |
| Even getting gas is more pleasant due to the lack of a gas cap. |
| Parallel parking no longer intimidates me thanks to self-parking. |
| The kids no longer fight in the backseats and are comfortable and quiet. |
| We have been able to fit anything we need in our vehicle. |
| *I really appreciate a good sound system and prefer 16 Bose speakers over just 8.* |
| *I prefer the performance of a V8 engine over a V6.* |
| *Power is important to me so I'd prefer 420 hp over 310 hp.* |

## SAFETY

| |
|---|
| This is the safest I have ever felt while driving any vehicle. |
| I no longer have costly repairs due to the best warranty available for my drive train. |
| I feel safer driving a vehicle with one of the highest rated crash test results. |
| *I prefer additional safety features such as Front and Read Park Assist, Surround Vision and Teen Driver technology.* |

## SALES EXPERIENCE –

| |
|---|
| I feel great knowing I am buying American and supporting American workers. |
| I know I bought a special luxury brand thanks to all the benefits I receive with Cadillac Shield. |
| I feel very confident in my purchase thanks to the A+ rating with the Better Business Bureau. |
| *I am comfortable spending $75,000 for a luxury vehicle of this quality.* |

Remember these four questions that Tim answered for me?

1. **What is the number one car people come in and say they want to buy?**
2. **What car is the car that all the salespeople dream of selling?**
3. **What features does that dream car have that no other cars have?**
4. **What are some quotes from happy customers that bought the dream car?**

The reason I asked these questions was to compare the vehicle that most people THINK they want to the vehicle most salespeople dream of selling.

As you may have noticed, the last few statements in the tables were shaded, bolded, and italicized. These statements are specific to the Escalade versus the XT5. The responses to those last few statements will indicate if the customer is actually considering the correct vehicle!

This leads me to the reason I originally decided to write a Visnostic Special Edition for Auto Sales...THE UPSELL!!

HOW TO USE VISNOSTICS TO UPSELL CUSTOMERS

If you have a customer walk in and say, *"I have done my research and I know what vehicle I'm interested in. I want to test drive your most popular vehicle which is the **Cadillac XT5**."*

Instead of allowing your "Order Taking" approach to kick in, try this instead...

*"**Great! Educated Clients are the BEST Clients! But before we test drive it, I am going to make five statements and please tell me which of these three responses best describe how you feel:**"*

- ***I can say this today***
- ***I WISH I could say this today or***
- ***It's not important"***

1. ***I really appreciate a good sound system and prefer 16 Bose speakers over just 8.***
2. ***I prefer the performance of a V8 engine over a V6.***
3. ***Power is important to me so I'd prefer 420 hp over 310 hp.***

4. *I prefer additional safety features such as Front and Read Park Assist, Surround Vision and Teen Driver technology.*
5. *I am comfortable spending $75,000 for a luxury vehicle of this quality.*

If you get a lot of "It's not important" responses than you should proceed to the XT5 test drive. But if they seem excited and answer with I WISH I could say this today, you should encourage them to test drive the Escalade before they drive the XT5.

Are you going to upsell every client? NO! But how many upsells have you done this month? I predict your zero will go WAY up. And if you are already upselling, I predict you will at least double what you are doing today! Email me your results!

Reach out to me and I will be thrilled to help you write the best Visnostic Statements for what YOU sell!

# SALES MANAGERS –
# HOW TO USE VISNOTICS TO HIRE YOUR COMPETITORS BEST SALESPEOPLE –

And then finally, what if you want to recruit top talent? What types of Visnostic Statements would differentiate your dealership from the competition? If you are a sales manager, please contact me and I will personally help you change the way you interview, advertise, recruit, and retain great salespeople! I would start out by interviewing your current staff. What are their favorite things about working for YOU? What are their favorite things about working for YOUR Dealership? You may want to come back to this exercise after you learn about RTH on the next page.

This special edition is not intended to replace *VISNOSTIC SALES AND MARKETING*. Instead, its purpose is to teach you just enough to make a positive impact with your communications style today. What will separate the Superstars from the other Auto Salespeople will be that hunger to get even better at this new communication style. Those of you with strong ambition will want to advance to the next level by reading *VISNOSTIC SALES AND MARKETING* or contacting DynaExec to setup a workshop for your team.

*VISNOSTIC SALES AND MARKETING* has two entire chapters dedicated to creating the absolute most powerful Visnostic Statements. But for this shorter version of the book, here is a synopsis –

# RTH

I'm actually using an acronym here to prove a point. Do you realize how overused acronyms are today? From a Visnostic perspective, it is the biggest mistake made today in Corporate America's sales and marketing departments. The chances are high that you will not remember the letters or what order they came in and your clients won't either. This is exactly why I wish manufacturers would go back to naming all their vehicles things like Escalade instead of XT5!!

Example – Recently, I was having a conversation with a reader and she kept using the acronym MSA. Coming from the software world, MSA stood for Master Service Agreement so I was having a really difficult time following the points she was making. It wasn't until well into the conversation that I asked what MSA meant in her world and it meant Marketing Specialist Agencies. Visnostics would have really helped our conversation!

**One of the most powerful messages Visnostic evangelizes is that we must avoid making our clients TRANSLATE our message.** Acronyms force the client to translate what they stand for so we must stop that madness!

From a Visnostic perspective, these three graphics are a better way to help you learn and retain the information. Can you guess the meaning of these three images?

Go back to the second step in writing Visnostic Statements. Look at the first few BOLDED words a few pages ago. Can you figure out what those first few words attempted to articulate? Here are some examples:

**SAVE MONEY**
**FEEL SUCCESSFUL**
**DRIVERS MOVE QUICKLY**
**PASSING IS EFFORTLESS**
**SMOOTH AND AIRY RIDE**
**NEVER GET INTO A HOT OR COLD CAR AGAIN**
**DRIVING IN WINTER WEATHER IS A BREEZE**
**NEVER TOUCH A GAS CAP AGAIN**
**PARALELL PARK LIKE A PRO EVERYTIME**

**ELIMINATE ALL THE CHARGING CORDS**
**YOUR FRIENDS WILL LOVE FOR YOU TO DRIVE**

These are the RESULTS clients receive from all the "Vendor Speak" that is out there! These are the words CLIENTS typically use when they describe why they like their vehicles. So why aren't we SELLING these RESULTS?!

# ANSWER: RTH =

RESULTS       TIMELINE       HOW

In a perfect world, you would have details such as "I saved $10,000 (RESULT) my first year (TIMELINE) in service charges due to the exceptional warranty (HOW)" is much more impactful than "I saved $10,000 over four years…" See why including timelines can be impactful?

As you learned from the Introduction, Simon Sinek's book, *Start With Why* points out that most marketing messaging starts out with the "What" and "How" companies do things. Instead, messaging should start out with WHY because that is the real reason clients buy.

Remember Tim's responses to my four questions? Remember how much those responses sounded like Marketing wrote them? (aka VENDOR– Speak). I attempted to translate those features, functions, and marketing jargon into WHY CLIENTS CARE (aka CLIENT–Speak). As I read about each feature online,

I was trying to convert them into the results, how quickly I would get those results, and then the feature is typically the HOW.

Examples –
"V8 Engine" is a feature. "Drivers move quickly" is the RESULT.
"Affordable Luxury" is a feature. "Save Money" is the RESULT.
"Four–Wheel–Drive" is a feature. "Driving in Winter Weather is a breeze" is a RESULT.

When writing results, the more details you have, the more impactful your statements will be. For example, everywhere I looked, it said Cadillac was the best value in its luxury category. But I couldn't find out HOW MUCH! This is where I encourage every salesperson to work with marketing to flush out these details. If a Cadillac and an equivalent Mercedes SUV were being compared, how much less money is the Cadillac? $10k? $20k? or $2k? These details make a huge difference to the Consumer. Most of them are trying to figure this out themselves. Do the work for them and they will be your fan!

When people are new at creating Visnostic Statements, they tend to focus on FEATURE/HOW things are done. This is a natural way we communicate because this approach is rampant in most messaging today. But it's INEFFECTIVE and we MUST fix it!

And I believe the students of Visnostics are going to change that for the better!

## I want to make a very strong point that not all Visnostic Statements are going to have

## Results and Timelines
## but the ones that have these components
## will often end up being
## your very best ones.

The best way for you to prove this point to yourself is to try some of them with your clients. Write as many as you can and invite your best client to lunch. Ask him or her to respond but to also let you know which ones resonated and triggered the most emotion. Mix in some Visnostics that have results and timelines with the statements that omitted them. Their reactions to them will validate this claim.

## Remember that a Visnostic Statement is not a
## promise or claim that you can do something.
## It is a way to help uncover what is important
## to your client.

------

# CLIENT-SPEAK VERSUS VENDOR-SPEAK

This is the most important point I want to make in this Special Edition for Auto Sales:

You learned about "Fight, Flight, or Freeze" in Chapter One; it is a normal neurological reaction to avoid salespeople. Too many salespeople start out with who they are and what their products can do. We can't do that anymore. Clients want to know "How can you make my life better?" And you only have 3–8 seconds to answer that question!

Don't waste that precious time using words like "We," "I," or "Me!" If your first three words don't start with RESULTS and using the word "YOU" instead of "I" that Fight/Flight gets turned on.

Simon Sinek is right – start with WHY. WHY they should care! And the RESULTS are why they care!

So if you use words like "I," "my," "our," "we," or "they" and you are talking size of engines, cubic square feet of cargo space, using fancy marketing words that only you understand, bragging about your company, using acronyms, industry jargon, gas mileage, and any other comments around the features and functions of the automobiles you are selling, **YOU ARE TALKING VENDOR-SPEAK!**

And I promise you that you ARE losing sales by doing this!

You simply cannot rely on your audience to translate all those "things" you think are so important into **WHY THEY CARE!**

# YOU MUST TRANSLATE FOR THEM!

In contrast, if you are using words like "you," "customers," or "owners," and you tell stories about other positive customer experiences, give examples how other owners have benefited, and leverage Visnostics to help them know what they REALLY want then **YOU ARE TALKING CLIENT-SPEAK** and they will love you for it because they don't have to work so hard to figure out why they should buy from you!

The final experiment I did for this book was to reach out to my contacts on social media and I asked this simple question –

*Please describe why you purchased your last vehicle. (Client-Speak). Also please include the make and model of your auto because I will look up the way the vehicle is marketed (Vendor-Speak) and compare your description to the way marketing describes it.*

I highlighted examples of Client–Speak in each example and then I researched how the manufacturers articulated the same thing.

Which form of communication do you think will resonate better with a potential client?

Here are some examples of those responses:

## CLIENT SPEAK EXAMPLE #1 -

Response from a first-time buyer:

*Honda Civic coupe 2015*

*I got this car in 2015 and it was my first car purchase ever.*

*I just moved to LA and lived my first three months without a car.*

*I had to take the bus, ride a bicycle or take Uber/Lyft.*

*I was spending like 600 bucks a month on Lyft – I even got an email from Lyft saying I was a top customer and that's when I knew I was spending too much on transportation.*

*I thought I wanted a yellow Toyota car because it was sporty and cool but when I stepped inside, I realized it was really antiquated in terms of features and technology and also really small and more expensive.*

*When I first saw the Civic, I didn't even know it was a Honda. I was shocked 'is this really a Honda? It looks so sleek and like a spaceship.'*

*I realized that I would be spending most of my time INSIDE the car so the features were really important.*

*I'm a tech savvy guy so I loved how futuristic the interior was designed with the dashboard. I loved that I could connect my iPhone to Bluetooth so that I can play my music and podcasts easily.*

*One of the most important features to me is that it has a second camera to help you see blind spots.*

*I don't need to turn my head to check my right side for blind spots– I just use my turn signal and I can see if anyone is in my blind spot. It's so useful, especially at nighttime on a freeway. I thought and still think it's such a life saving feature to save me from any accidents.*

*This blind spot camera is not even available for other cars, even high–end cars like Lexus or BMW! So I thought wow I can't believe only Honda has this in their cars.*

*A lot of people have been impressed by it and surprised that it's not available on other more expensive cars.*

*I could finally get to work and not have to ride a bicycle at night when it's so dark and potentially get hit. I also didn't have to bother my co-workers for a ride home.*

*I could save money from not using Uber and Lyft so much. I can have the freedom to go anywhere I want and can bring anyone else. I could pick up a girl for a date or drive her back home.*

*I can also put my pool cues in my trunk as well as other miscellaneous stuff so I can have it on me at all times.*

*I also put some emergency stuff like first aid kits, rations, water, flashlight, etc. in case of a natural disaster.*

Can you see that what this owner is describing are the RESULTS of a feature? Can you also see the various segmentations? I see "Safety" – "help you see blind spots." I also see "Driver Experience" – It was "sporty and cool" and "sleek like a spaceship" are just a couple of segmentation examples.

I found several pre-owned versions of this exact car for sale online and no matter how many times I see things marketed this way, it still boggles my mind.

Why in the world would anybody want to buy this vehicle based upon the following description? This single example should drive (pun) home the points about Visnostics!

**We must TRANSLATE these features and functions into why our customers actually make buying decisions!!**

This is how an advertisement articulated these same features using **VENDOR-SPEAK EXAMPLE #1 –**
Can you finally see the "YUK" in this communication style?

| FEATURES | | | | |
|---|---|---|---|---|
| BROCHURE | **Engine Type** | 1.8L I4 | **MPG** | 30 City / 39 Hwy |
| WARRANTY | **Exterior Color** | Dk. Gray | **Interior Color** | Gray |
| | **Transmission** | Automatic, CVT | **Drivetrain** | FWD |
| | **Doors** | 4 Door Sedan | **Number of Keys** | 1 |
| | **Seating** | 5 Passenger | **VIN** | 19XFB2F53FE256961 |
| | **Stock #** | 2000350207 | **Vehicle ID** | 1262025 |

| | | |
|---|---|---|
| **BRAKING AND TRACTION** | · Traction Control<br>· ABS (4-Wheel) | · Stability Control |
| **COMFORT AND CONVENIENCE** | · Alarm System<br>· Air Conditioning<br>· Power Door Locks | · Keyless Entry<br>· Power Windows<br>· Cruise Control |
| **STEERING** | · Power Steering | · Tilt & Telescoping Wheel |
| **ENTERTAINMENT AND INSTRUMENTATION** | · AM/FM Stereo<br>· Bluetooth Wireless | · CD/MP3 (Single Disc) |
| **SAFETY AND SECURITY** | · Backup Camera<br>· Side Air Bags | · Dual Air Bags<br>· F&R Head Curtain Air Bags |
| **LIGHTING** | · Daytime Running Lights | |
| **WHEELS AND TIRES** | · Steel Wheels | |

## CLIENT SPEAK EXAMPLE #2 -

Response from an experienced buyer:

*Tesla Model–S 2018*
*I recently bought a Tesla Model S (about a year ago). My previous vehicle had been getting older.*
*The criteria for the new vehicle was:*
*It needed to be appropriate to my position in life, and reflect the high–tech aspect of our business. (We have a high–tech company, so it makes most sense to have a high–tech car).*
*We considered a Land–Rover and a Tesla Model–S and Porche advertised it is coming out with an all–electric vehicle.*
*A serious concern I have is that we humans are seriously harming the planet with all the gasoline we are burning, it is likely a major contributing factor to global climate change which science says is all too likely to bring on an irreversible major hardship the kind of which we should not wish on future generations. In addition, the price of gasoline that we in the USA pay is artificially held down (as I realized when traveling in Europe where it is not held down so artificially – it seemed about $8–$9gallon there), and so at any time the price of gas could easily become several times what we pay.*
*All this gave a strong preference to an electric–powered car.*
*There are a lot of electric cars on the market, but most do not correctly reflect my position in life.*
*And \*none\* of them really have solid range to drive from SFO to LA, over 300 miles.*
*Only Tesla has a workable solution (although requiring purchase of their high–end battery which adds $20k to the price), which is what they call "Superchargers" several locations from here to LA, which can charge the battery in about an hour. Located often with a good restaurant nearby, one can start the car charging and eat lunch, and back to the car in about the*

same time as charging is done. This is a crucial feature — who wants to buy a car then not be able to go on family trips?

This Tesla is a full-size sedan (not the cheaper smaller Model-3), with the power of a high-end Porche. Press the accelerator and you are going the speed you want within literally 2 seconds, which makes driving on the freeway in traffic significantly easier. This kind of acceleration is often associated with wasteful "manliness" but it has a very practical aspect (and my wife loves to drive this car).

If you know the price of this car, you know that price was *not* my biggest concern. And I could have gotten a more "luxurious" car, but that would be gas-burning.

Made in USA was not a deal-breaker for the other cars, but is a plus for Tesla.

## VENDOR SPEAK EXAMPLE #2 -

I went to Tesla's website and I was stunned how they marketed their vehicles. I was expecting it to be in alignment with Client Speak but it was full of statistics, features, functions, and other specs. Because of the copyright of their website, I won't paste screen shots in this book but I encourage you to go look at their website. I'm sending a copy of this book to Elon Musk!

https://www.tesla.com/inventory/new/ms

**2.4 sec**
0-60 mph

**163 mph**
Top Speed

**345 mi**
Range (EPA)

**Featured Options**

- Model S Performance
- Pearl White Multi-Coat
- All Black Interior with Carbon Fiber Decor
- 19" Silver Wheels
- Full Self-Driving Capability
- Glass Roof

# Conclusion

You should now be able to see how Visnostic Statements can strengthen your marketing content. What blows my mind is how difficult it is to change these bad behaviors!

There have been many books written throughout the years attempting to change or improve the ways products are marketed. Yet everybody continues to do it the same old way because, just like the "roast" story I told in the Introduction of this book, nobody questions it. Buyers don't question it and neither do the Sellers. If you want to be innovative, if you want to make a difference, why not try something new?

## Remember, your competitors are reading this book as well! The "winner" will be the dealerships that embrace VISNOSTICS FIRST!

Visnostics destroy the insanity that is taking place with all the features and functions being advertised in an attempt to sell cars! I want to leave you with one final story:

I bought this car in 2001 and paid cash thanks to a pretty good commission check. And yes, I used Visnostics to win the business. I just didn't fully understand the science behind what I was doing yet.

Here is the original advertisement I saw online and the history of why we bought it:

1966 AC Shelby Cobra hybrid (part replica/part original)
Air conditioning was added to the Cobra
1.1 k miles
Larry Lingenfelter built 390 cubic inch,
FE Block Tremec 5-speed
Flawless pearl blue and white stripes
Black leather embroidered seats imported from Italy
Boyd Coddington wheels
Ceramic coated headers and pipes
Chrome Aldan shocks
Complete engine dress kit

I was getting concerned; my husband had Auto Trader magazines lying all around our house. One day, I flipped through one to see what types of cars he had dog-eared and I was appalled to see old muscle cars that needed a LOT of work. I envisioned our HOA flipping out when my husband ended up with one of these cars in our driveway, up on blocks. I envisioned oil stains everywhere and a stinky and grumpy husband frustrated  as he tried to restore these classics to their glory. I also envisioned how expensive it was going to be and how long it was going to take. He obviously needed my help to find a GOOD car and keep our HOA from breathing down our necks!

So I went online and I found this beauty. I had no clue what all that stuff listed was about or why it mattered. All I knew is that it was gorgeous and I could tell it wasn't going to need any work done to it.

When my husband got home from work, I showed him this car and he said, "I have that car dog-eared!" And I said, "No you don't. I looked at all of your Auto Traders and I saw the cars you were looking at." He then pulled out a brand-new Auto Trader from his brief case and it was true – he had it dog-eared. WE BOTH LOVED THIS CAR!

I don't know which one of us was more surprised but because of this unusual alignment in taste, we HAD to go look at this car!

I was so sure I was going to buy it that I got a cashier's check and we got a trailer and drove two hours to look at it.

When we actually saw it in person, the look on my husband's face was priceless. But when the owner started the car, I was stunned how my body physically reacted; I actually got goose bumps! No car had ever affected me like that! The base sound from the exhaust pipes took my breath away! I envisioned how cool we would look driving this beauty around town! SOLD!

We have now had this car for over 18 years! Oh my gosh! I just realized how crazy that is! We baby this car. It stays in a garage and is covered. We hardly drive it and I actually got up from writing this to go see what our mileage is on the car and I even took a picture just for this conclusion.

This is going to make a lot of readers sick to see –

This car is obviously wasted on us! This means in 18 years, we have only driven this car 2,557.6 miles! That means we averaged about 142 miles per year. I am ashamed of us!
My husband said it sounds like it needs a new water pump so the past few times I've wanted to drive it, we can't. And other

times I have wanted to drive it, the inspection or tags were expired. So it's been sitting in the garage more than it's been on the road.

But when we DO get it out, WOW! First of all, every single time I drive it, my heart rate goes up because my adrenaline goes into over-drive. I have no idea why this happens. It hasn't happened with any other vehicle. I respect the power of this car. I won't even drink coffee if I'm going to drive it because I'm afraid I will have a heart attack!

When we drive it, people speed up to get next to us. We get dozens of "thumbs up" signs, people honk, wave, and SMILE! The biggest joy to me is how this car affects other people! It puts a huge smile on the faces of most people driving around us and I love that feeling.

One of our favorite things to do is to park the car in front of a restaurant patio, go eat on the patio and people-watch. What

I LOVE to see is when people take pictures standing around it and we will walk up to them and open the door and tell them to get in and we offer to take pictures of them. They get so excited! And that is so fun for us!

The reason that I just shared all of that in this book is to make my point about how to sell more autos! NOT ONCE DID I LIST ANYTHING ON THIS LIST AS REASONS I LOVE THIS CAR! So Stop selling like this –

1966 AC Shelby Cobra hybrid (part replica/part original)
Air conditioning was added to the Cobra
1.1 k miles
Larry Lingenfelter built 390 cubic inch,
FE Block Tremec 5-speed
Flawless pearl blue and white stripes
Black leather embroidered seats imported from Italy
Boyd Coddington wheels
Ceramic coated headers and pipes
Chrome Aldan shocks
Complete engine dress kit
Instead, sell like THIS –

**"You're feeling like a celebrity on this gorgeous 70-degree day; wind in your hair, people honking, waving, smiling, and taking pictures…You feel sexy, sassy, and FREE of any worries! Your adrenaline is flowing from the power of the 1966 AC Shelby Cobra you are driving. Life just doesn't get any better than this!"**

**Can YOU say this today?**
**Do you WISH you could say this today?**
**Or is it even important to you?**
**If you WISH you could say this today, call me at XXX.XXX.XXXX!**

You will be shocked how many more calls you will get! Paint a VISION of how your Buyer's life will be better and they will not only come to you, they will ASK you to sell to them! It is AFTER they come see you that you discuss all those Features and Functions. But only if and when they ASK!

I'm not saying that there isn't a NEED for the features and functions; **the problem is that salespeople and marketing rely on the Features and Functions and expect buyers to paint their visions in their head. But most of us are too lazy to do that! So we need to do it for them!**

Does this make sense? You will need to see it work to really understand the power of Visnostics!

## SO WHEN ARE YOU GOING TO TRY IT?

This mini-lesson, written exclusively for Auto Sales Professionals, is intended to give you a taste of what to expect from any of the books in the Visnostic Series.

There are two chapters dedicated to writing incredible Visnostic Statements. This entire book will be included as well. Which is a GOOD thing because repetition increases retention and comprehension! (See Introduction.)

But the major component that is missing from this mini-book is that the full books will teach you how to create actual sales tools that **will ensure new salespeople are confident and competent to interact with clients From their first few days selling!**

To learn more about developing powerful Visnostic Statements, and how to work with your existing clients to create the absolute best testimonials, please read any of the Visnostic Series by Kimberlee Slavik. The books are available in over 42,000 bookstores worldwide.

For information about scheduling workshops or keynote speaking at any of your business meetings, please email autosales@dynaexec.com.

# APPENDIX
## Sales Basics Review, Tips, and Answers

## Neuroscience Definition:

neu·ro·sci·ence

'n(y)o͞orō͵sīəns/

noun: **neuroscience**; plural noun: **neurosciences**

Any or all of the sciences, such as neurochemistry and experimental psychology, which deal with the structure or function of the nervous system and brain.

## Neuroscience References:

**Using Neuroscience to skyrocket sales**
https://neilpatel.com/blog/7-neuroscience-principles-you-should-use-to-increase-sales/
**Your Brain Prefers Cartoons over Photos**
https://www.newyorker.com/culture/culture-desk/this-is-your-brain-on-cartoons/amp
**Why Questions and Surveys annoy clients**
https://www.mycustomer.com/community/blogs/wizu/7-reasons-why-your-customers-hate-your-surveys
**The Neuroscience of Selling – INC magazine**
https://www.inc.com/geoffrey-james/the-neuroscience-of-selling.html
**What Great Salespeople Do Summary**
http://storyleaders.com/book/
**More Science**
https://blog.insidesales.com/inside-sales-thought-leaders/buyers-brain/

## Basic Sales Psychology Principles:

Sales rejection is partially due to human natures resistance to being persuaded. Winning a point or argument is what humans want and need.

## Body Language Basics:

**Looking to Their Right** = Auditory Thought (Remembering a song)

**Looking to Their Left** = Visual Thought (Remembering the color of a dress)

**Looking Down to Their Right** = Someone is creating a feeling or sensory memory (Thinking what it would be like to swim in Jell-O)

**Looking Down to Their Left** = Someone talking to themselves

## Pain Drives Buyers - Good Pain and Bad Pain:

People buy due to pain (GOOD pain is caused by things like rapid growth, lack of resources, supply chain issues, etc. and BAD pain is caused by things like no growth, layoffs necessary, too much stock, etc.) A good salesperson will be attempting to uncover pain throughout the sales process.

## Business Terminology:

**B2B – Business to Business –**

When a company sells to another company.

Example: A computer manufacturer will sell wholesale to a retail store versus the consumer.

**B2C – Business to Consumer –**

When a company sells to the end-user.

Example: When a retail store sells directly to the consumer.

**Some companies have distribution models that are both B2B and B2C.**

## Visnostic Book URL References:

**"You Are Who You Are Because Where You Were When"**
https://www.youtube.com/watch?v=_aY163kwlW4
**"7 Presentation Ideas That Work for Any Topic."**
https://www.inc.com/carmine-gallo/7-presentation-ideas-that-work-for-any-topic.html
**"The Rule of Threes"**
https://www.youtube.com/watch?v=SY23zi1u_3U
**SlideShare**
https://www.slideshare.net
**DynaExec Visnostic Statements**
https://www.surveymonkey.com/r/TR73SMS
**Kimberlee Slavik**
https://www.linkedin.com/in/kimslavik
**DynaExec Website Video**
https://player.vimeo.com/video/353714183
**David A. Wiener**
https://www.linkedin.com/in/david-a-wiener-573b1a1/
**David's artwork**
http://artbydavidwiener.blogspot.com

## The Art of Answering Questions:

Never ask closed-ended questions – Yes and No answers can be blurted out without any thought behind the answer. Open-ended questions have problems as well because they can go in many different directions and you lose focus on the original intent. Having multiple-choice is the best way for the audience to ponder and consider the options. They have to think harder to answer, which is how you get people emotionally engaged.

Studies have shown that giving people options, triggers chemicals in the brain to choose one. For example – if you say "Will you buy from me?" Yes or No? It is way too easy to say No. However, if you give your client THREE pricing/package options from which to choose, they will typically choose one. So it is an automatic YES. So when I am responded to an RFP (Request for Proposal), RFI (Request for Information, or an RFQ (Request for Quotation), I always provide three alternative pricing scenarios. The theory is that they will choose one of the three options vs. eliminating you from the other bids.

## Questions Continued - Very Important Point:

When a client asks a question, you will automatically want to answer it. Instead, ask what is driving that specific question. Often, the real question is not what the client actually asked. When I go on sales calls with a Software Engineer, Technical Support, Management, or other teammates, their purpose for being on the call is usually to answer all questions sales can't handle. However, when questions arise, it is imperative to uncover what is driving the question so you don't get drug down the wrong path and derail the momentum of the meeting.

For example, I was in a meeting about three weeks before Thanksgiving and the client asked what was the average implementation time. This is a logical question and my engineer wanted to tell the client that the answer was six weeks. Instead of answering the question, I asked the client why this question was important and they responded with they wanted to make sure it could be completed before the holidays (which I just said was in three weeks). If we had answered the question with the "six weeks" response, the client would have jumped to the conclusion that we were not the appropriate solution and we would have lost the sale.

The real question the client wanted to ask was, "Could you have this implemented by the holidays?" And our answer would have been, "Yes, we will double up on resources to ensure implementation is complete by the holidays."

## Company and book sites:

www.dynaexec.com
www.visnostics.com
www.visnosticselling.com

## Buy Books:

**Memoirs of an Angry Sales Pro – Sales Leadership MUST Change!**
https://www.amazon.com/Memoirs-Angry-Sales-Pro-Leadership/dp/1733194630/ref=sr_1_1?keywords=memoirs+of+an+angry+sales+pro&qid=1568169902&s=gateway&sr=8-1

**Visnostics Special Edition for Real Estate**
https://www.amazon.com/Visnostics-Neuroscientific-Approach-Communicating-Marketing/dp/1733194614/ref=sr_1_2?keywords=visnostic+selling&qid=1566930437&s=gateway&sr=8-2

**Visnostics Special Edition for Auto Sales**

https://www.amazon.com/Visnostics-VISualization-DiagNOSTIC-Neuroscientific-Communicating/dp/1733194649/ref=sr_1_3?keywords=visnostic+selling&qid=1566930437&s=gateway&sr=8-3

**Visnostic Selling
(Replaced with Visnostic Sales and Marketing)**
https://www.amazon.com/Visnostic-Selling-neuroscientific-marketing-leadership/dp/1732191611/ref=sr_1_1?keywords=visnostic+selling&qid=1566930399&s=gateway&sr=8-1

## Podcasts and Other URLs:
**Visnostic Podcasts, Education, and Speaking:**

**July 19, 2019** – Donald C. Kelly, The Sales Evangelist
The Fundamentals of Visnostic Selling
https://www.stitcher.com/podcast/donald-kelly/the-sales-evangelist-sales-trainingspeakingbusiness-marketingdonald/e/62674347

**June 18, 2019** – Brian Burns, The Brutal Truth About
Sales Basic Visnostics – Statements NOT Questions
https://www.stitcher.com/podcast/brian-burns/the-brutal-truth-about-sales-selling/e/61931321?autoplay=true

**April 22, 2019** – Dr. Pelè, Big Ticket Clients
Basic Visnostics
https://www.youtube.com/watch?v=FbW-sSu4BOo&t=304s

**Current CEO DynaExec Introduction to Visnostics**

https://player.vimeo.com/video/353714183

**Visnostics in Seven Seconds**
https://www.youtube.com/watch?v=dy5s4kYWdjY.

# WORKSHOPS

In addition to Fractional Leadership that can be contracted for a day, week, month, quarter, or an entire year, there are three workshops that help DynaExec clients execute three major principles taught in the best-selling book, *Visnostic™ Sales & Marketing*.

First, vendor-centric marketing messaging must be translated and converted into client-centric Visnostic Statements. This is accomplished by working with sales and marketing during a **Translation Workshop**. This is the fundamental workshop needed to create stronger messaging. This workshop eliminates the need for clients to translate features and functions and other jargon into "why they care." This is accomplished by doing the work for them. This workshop converts current messaging into dialogue that will improve your clients' comprehension and retention of your messaging.

In addition, you will strengthen your rapport with your clients because they will FEEL positive emotions while engaging with your sales organization. Your sales organization will be able to quickly identify the clients' non-strength areas in which your company can convert to strengths.

Once the translation is completed and 10-20 strong "Visnostic Statements" are created per segmentation, the next step is the **Solution Mapping Workshop**. This second workshop is conducted with a more technical team while reviewing the Visnostic Statements created during the Translation Workshop.

Often, these second sets of eyes will identify and create additional Visnostic Statements to the ones Sales and Marketing identified during the Translation Workshop. In addition, this second group tend to enhance the newly created statements with powerful results they have observed during their post sales efforts. These final Visnostic Statements are then mapped to various Statement of Work descriptions that will describe HOW any "non-strengths" uncovered during the client discussion can become strengths. These Statement of Work descriptions are created during the Solution Mapping Workshop.

The final stage of the Visnostic transformation is to take the Visnostic Statements and the Statement of Works and complete a tool that will be given to the entire sales organization. Imagine a sales team that is in front of the client with a tablet, documenting the client responses. And residing on the tablet is a tool that will automatically produce an "Insight Report" that will give your clients a recipe for success INSTANTLY!

This will eliminate the need for technical resources to be engaged early in the sales cycle. The client will see exactly how your company will turn their non-strengths into strengths!

The third workshop is **Visnostic Selling**, which is conducted with the entire sales organization to ensure they are each experts with the tool and they are well prepared to properly engage with the client.

## Your sales organization will be CONFIDENT and COMPETENT in front of potential clients from their first WEEK in their sales role!

Here are the three workshops in greater detail -

## ★ Client-Centric Translation For Sales & Marketing

### Objective –
Conversion is a form of translation. Converting features and functions into VISualization DiagNOSTIC (aka Visnostic) Statements is the act of translating vendor-centric wording (vendor-speak) into client-centric statements (client-speak) that clients can relate. DynaExec will assess current marketing tools & combine details from multiple sources to create Visnostic Statements & compatible visuals & graphics that enhance retention.

### Attendees –
Sales and Marketing (Up to twelve participants)

### Pre-requisites, Planning, and Preparation for Workshop –
- **Read _Visnostic Selling_ Book** – (Preface, Chapters 1-3) Retail Price - $24.95 Workshop Discounted Rate - $19.95

- **Meeting #1** – Assessment - Conference Call to hear Presentation & Record for transcription (obtain script)
- **Meeting #2** – Assessment Results Revealed. Kick-off conference call after book is read but prior to workshop to set expectations
- **Meeting #3** – Onsite 8-hour Translation Workshop
  - ✓ CHAPTER ONE – Believing is Doing and Introduction (30 minutes)
  - ✓ Exercise #1 – "XXXX" exercise.
  - ✓ Slide presentation using graphics vs words
  - ✓ 3 graphics versus letters exercise – 3 seconds per slide Generation Z get timer added to PPT
  - ✓ CHAPTER TWO – Segmentation and why it is important. (30 minutes)
  - ✓ CHAPTER THREE – Solution Dissection. (1 hour)
  - ✓ CHAPTER FOUR – Translation (1 hour)
  - ✓ CHAPTER FIVE – Creating & Rating Visnostic Statements with Post It Notes by Segmentation. The importance of RTH. Use highlighters to identify, Reword if necessary. Prioritize. (1 hour working lunch)
  - ✓ CHAPTER SIX – Vertical and Target Market Strategies with Visnostic Statements (1 hour)
  - ✓ CHAPTER SEVEN – Class Presentations. Time will be determined based upon number of companies in each session and flexibility of class.
  - ✓ CHAPTER EIGHT – Conclusion and discussion of two additional workshops to create the tool. Demo of tool.
- **Ongoing Meetings (up to 30 days)** – Ensure success and document results are included in the workshop price.

**Supplies Needed for In-Person Workshop –**
- Conference Room with projection and white board
- Phone for call-in participants
- Internet
- Post-it Notes supplied by DynaExec
- Highlighters supplied by DynaExec

---

# ★ Mapping Segmentation Solution Workshop for Post Sales Roles

**Objective –**
After the feedback from the client is collected, a deliverable must be created that maps all "NON-STRENGTHS" identified with Visnostic Statements. It is important to not simply map products or services names to the areas in which can be strengthened. This workshop will summarize HOW your company will help clients improve their current situations. The result will be a client deliverable called an Insight Report.

**Attendees –**
Technical Team such as Software Engineers, Implementers, Support, Compliance, etc. (Up to twelve participants)

---

# ★ Visnostic Sales and Marketing Workshop

**Objective –**
After the first two workshops, a sales tool will be completed that converted features/functions and other technical jargon into statements the client can reflect and visualize. Sales will learn how to deliver this approach in lieu of a traditional sales

presentation. Sales will learn how to use the new tool designed to create the Client Insight Report. Sales people need to be entertained to learn. This workshop will have games and prizes as a shorter version of both previous workshops is conducted to ensure the sales organization understands basic Visnostics and the science behind why it works so well.

**Attendees –**
Sales and Sales Leadership (Up to twelve participants)
In less than 30 days and three workshops, with Visnostic Selling, your sales, marketing, and leadership will be transformed into Client Business Strategists. Furthermore, your clients will no longer avoid your teams' sales efforts because they will be viewed as a valuable extension of your client's own teams.

---

## ★ Additional Information

Workshops can be conducted in public forums or in private sessions.

The benefit of group forums is that during your presentation to the group, you will be educating other companies on the benefits, results, and differentiators of your company, which could result in new clients.

TIP – Companies that send representatives from both marketing and sales will benefit the most from the Translation Workshop, which is the most popular and fundamental way to strengthen the effectiveness of the messaging.

---

## ★ Assessment of Current Messaging – Pricing Options

**ASSESSMENT** - $1,500
This includes approximately 10 hours of consulting work prior to the in-person workshop. Cost of the Assessment will be applied to any future consulting services and workshops.

1. Read at the minimum, Preface and Chapters 1-3. (2 hours)
2. Record your best presentation (30 min max) on Zoom with slides.
3. Transcribe the presentation. (3 – 5 hours)
4. Bring four different highlighter pens (blue, yellow, pink, and green are preferred).
5. Be prepared to discuss your top five differentiators over your competition. (1 hour of research)
6. Download app – Poll Everywhere

**POST WORKSHOP** - $500/month retainer for consulting services.

*Visnostic Sale and Marketing* Readers and Pod Cast audience may contact podcast@DynaExec.com for *a free assessment ($1,500 value).\**

**When was the last time you purchased a $25 book and received $1,500 of consulting for FREE?**
**\*Special Pricing is for a Limited Time Only**

---

# BIOGRAPHIES
## Author Bio and Resumé

## Kimberlee Slavik –
https://www.linkedin.com/in/kimslavik

Kimberlee is an award-winning business strategist in the Information Technology (IT) industry, known for helping clients increase sales and profits by leveraging software, services, hardware, storage, business continuity, & cloud computing.

Currently CEO of DynaExec.
Member of several advisory boards.

**Results:**
- ✓ Sold or participated in selling over $1.9 billion worth of software, products, & services during a 30-year career
- ✓ Best Selling Author and inventor of Visnostic Selling Series
- ✓ Exceeded quota for 26 years of a 30-year career averaging almost 200% of plan
- ✓ Award Winning Global Sales Leader
- ✓ Over 85 unsolicited recommendations on LinkedIn from clients, peers, direct reports, indirect reports, and management validating accomplishments
- ✓ Exceeded $900 million-dollar revenue objectives while managing a complex, 70+ person storage team with P&L (Profit and Loss) accountability for HP
- ✓ Recipient of numerous sales awards by focusing on post-sales support and customer references

**Specialties:**
- ✓ Surpassing sales objectives
- ✓ Inspirational Leadership Style
- ✓ Marketing and Sales Liaison
- ✓ Expert at selling intangible offerings
- ✓ Excellent post-sales client relationships
- ✓ Member of multiple advisory boards
- ✓ Training and education development and execution
- ✓ Transforming salespeople into top performers
- ✓ Exceptional business acumen & P&L (Profit and Loss)
- ✓ 15 years of people leadership
- ✓ Excellent communication & presentation skills
- ✓ Key Note Speaker
- ✓ Collaborative team player leading multiple teams towards a common goal
- ✓ Project management & organizational skills
- ✓ Organizational design & coaching high-performance teams
- ✓ Enterprise channel strategy development & execution
- ✓ C-level executives & senior execs sales closures
- ✓ Indirect enterprise channel sales & marketing
- ✓ Expertise in technology – including SaaS (Software as a Service), cloud, storage, virtualization, & business continuity

**Education:**
- ✓ Summa Cum Laude from LeTourneau University, with a Bachelor of Science degree in Business Administration.
- ✓ Certified by Southern Methodist University in "Leading the High-Performance Sales Organization."
- ✓ Currently pursuing an MBA degree in International Business at Heriot-Watt Business School in Edinburgh, Scotland.

# Foreword Bio and Resumé

**Joseph Ingram –**
https://www.linkedin.com/in/joeingram/

Joe Ingram is the creator of the "Genius Training System."

He is a husband first, father second, and he is also a best-selling author and an industry leader in both the automotive and software industries. He is known for helping clients increase both sales and profitability in all departments within the dealership walls. Joe has personally managed several single rooftop dealerships to over 1,000 units sold per month. He also trains many of the number one dealerships in the united states and overseas. With the average franchise dealership in the united states selling less than 100 units per month, Joe has consistently 10x'd the average. Joe is known for two things, always improving dealerships results in both fixed and variable operations, and he and his team deliver the training and instruction utilizing humor. The term Edu-tainment is applicable – the fusion of education and entertainment.

A highly accomplished 25-year sales veteran, Joe has held leadership roles for automotive industry leaders such as AutoNation, DealerSocket, I-Magic lab, and the Joe Verde Group. With extensive knowledge in human psychology, buying triggers, and e-commerce conversions, he can transform your results within months, not years. Joe has a passion for converting virtual prospects into sold units. His training incorporates varied communication styles, assumed rapport strategies, and real-world terminology to get more opportunities into the showroom for delivery. Understanding that customer satisfaction is a critical factor in retaining the customer you worked so hard to sell, Joe's clients continuously see a massive uplift in factory scores and social media reviews. Within six months of assuming control of an import dealership in Southern California, Joe and his team increased unit sales by 51% year over year, increased service volume and revenue by 100%, and maintained #1 rankings in both Sales and Service Satisfaction score for the western region.

Joe is a Southern California native and currently resides in Orange County with his bride of 20 years (who runs the number 1 Jeep dealership in California). He and his trainers provide their clients exceptional results all over the united states, both in-person and virtually.

# Artist Bio and Resumé

## David A. Wiener –
https://www.linkedin.com/in/david-a-wiener-573b1a1/

David is an action-oriented generalist with diverse sales and marketing experience in high technology environments. After engineering design and system installation of cryogenic systems, he entered the selling world of investment brokerage of large apartment buildings.

Then, after a decade of real estate investment, he moved to the high-tech industry. He has a strong focus on business start-up, market expansion, and turnaround situations. He demonstrated success in sales and sales management of system and application software as well as hardware. He has been successful at small and large companies and divisions of large companies starting new ventures. He has held positions up to and including VP Sales. He has held a TS clearance and has expertise with systems integrators and government programs.

After his career in high tech, David moved on to small farm communities in Florida, Texas and then upstate New York where he built a studio and produces his art of fine ink drawings, oil paintings, and ceramics. He also spends his time working for his town as chair of the planning board. He also is a member of the County planning board and a board member of the town fire department.

Education: Newark College of Engineering - BSME, MSIE, MSCIS (abt)


For more information about David's artwork or to commission his talent, please visit http://artbydavidwiener.blogspot.com

www.ingramcontent.com/pod-product-compliance
Lightning Source LLC
Chambersburg PA
CBHW050110210326
41519CB00015BA/3904